THE GUAVA TREE

RUTH MCALLISTER,
THE FOREST GIRL

WESTBOW
PRESS®
A DIVISION OF THOMAS NELSON
& ZONDERVAN

WestBow Press books may be ordered through booksellers or by contacting:

WestBow Press
A Division of Thomas Nelson & Zondervan
1663 Liberty Drive
Bloomington, IN 47403
www.westbowpress.com
844-714-3454

ISBN: 978-1-6642-6076-4 (sc)
ISBN: 978-1-6642-6075-7 (e)

Print information available on the last page.

WestBow Press rev. date: 03/28/2022

This story is dedicated to all my forest friends who didn't make it

PREFACE

To Ruth...for you were always Home, even when you couldn't find it.

The Journey
With furtive steps, and hopes and dreams
We found ourselves on paths unseen
Not yet trod, like fresh felled snow
To follow what the soul shall sow
To walk the paths of righteousness
With outstretched arms I start my quest
Removing mask and well-worn scars
And lies and my pretends
My footsteps mark my journey's past
But not my journey's end
And what I found
I always knew
I'm here to serve
Both me and you
And trust and know, that I'm enough
Not hide behind the gleaming stuff
To live and die, and once more live
To gratefully receive and humbly give
To be splayed unto my very core
I stand and climb and fly and soar

To know my voice will speak Thy truth
I forge and hone once timeless roots

With furtive steps
New hope, old dreams
I pause on pathways now revealed
In my direction I must go
No longer fast, just lifetime slow
I've opened to your world above
Awakened soul
Awake to Love
To climb, take shelter in Your Tree
Where You were hung, some say for me
To find my rest, to see Your face
To feel encircled by Your Grace
No longer need I run from me
Or climb atop that Guava Tree
My heart, my Light, my future's past
Has now come Home
To me at last

Rosie

Thank you, Rosie, my "twinster", for your amazing poem.
We are twins who understand the world in very similar ways
and who hear each other's voice in this world.

CHAPTER ONE

THE VIEW FROM A TREE

Facing a firing squad and I was only 4. I remember that day like it was yesterday. Guns in our faces, why? Does God really love the whole world? My life has been an amazing unfolding of learning and growing in understanding. I have been learning who I am and how I fit in this world and really how much God actually does love this world.

My earliest memories involve trees. I have always thought about my memories in terms of trees: those that are strong and tall, others that seem to offer no real use and still others that have a practical nature and something quite significant to offer. Since I was very young, I have recognized the significance of trees as partners in the circle of life as well as observers of that life. In fact, when I see a landscape void of trees, it seems that so much has been lost, not captured and definitely not shared. You see, trees are alive and often have lives for such a long time. It is comforting to know that trees connect generations and make sense of what we experience in our duration of life – if I live for around 80 or 90 years, that is wonderful. Trees I share that life span with, however, and who have been here for hundreds of years, make connections I could never make – often even for families. To know that your children will play where you played and your parents and their parents played, brings a wonderful sense of longevity and reminds us that no life is wasted, and memories can be remembered for a very long time and by many people. The reason, of course, that trees can live so long is because of their roots; the stronger the root system of a tree, the longer and more healthy its life. I've always admired that there is as much going on below the ground for trees as above.

So why does that impact me so profoundly? Well, my life has no roots; I am a person of many places and even more surroundings and contexts of life. Many new beginnings and even more endings. In fact, "hello and goodbye" have been said in my life so often and to so many people and places that I even have come to dread any more "hellos".

In a sense, I am the antithesis to a good tree and perhaps why I find so much to admire in them – I have longed for most of my life to be recognized and accepted as from somewhere and for belonging. Yet, what is amazing is that I was born in a forest, thick with trees - the Ituri Forest in the center of Africa. I was not only born in the center of the world, but also surrounded by trees. So, while I have been searching for roots in my own life, I was born surrounded by the most rooted of all living things - a thick forest of trees.

As I unwind my story here, you will see with me that my life has had many scopes and many contexts. I am a person of this earth in one sense as every human is and we're reminded by the minister when folk die, "From earth we came and to the earth we return." Yet, in quite another sense I resemble more of the nomadic earth dweller. Like those ancients who were constantly on the move. My father told me that he remembers me always talking about traveling and living in different countries. In fact, I remember having a list. I often said, as a teenager, "I want to live in Canada, the USA and Switzerland." Now, while that seems a random list, as I will explain, I have, in fact, lived in those countries along with others and there has always been a good reason why. That is interesting to me. The more you live life, the more connections you appreciate and the more you begin to wonder about the reasons for things. Getting back to trees for a moment…

There are different types of trees with different functions – just like people in a way. Some trees are pretty to look at but really do not offer any kind of functionality beyond that (apart from the generic support of our atmosphere, which is highly significant as we know). Other trees are really old and help us remember. Other, less ancient trees, the practical trees, offer a service - for their fruit or use as ornaments or for their wood, or protection. I found that kind of a tree when I was quite young. It stood in a small orchard that had been planted by people years before my time but for a specific service – to bear fruit. It was a puny orchard with only a few trees but there was one special tree, a Guava tree, which stood not too tall from the ground which meant that I could reach up and climb it easily. I was 7 years old and lived in the country then called Zaire, now called the Democratic Republic of the Congo (DRCongo) in Africa. Its bows weren't too large either and the lower limbs had just the right bend and shape to reach down to me and let me pull myself up into their sway. Just like "Baby Bear" in fact, I felt like it was "just right".

I went to my tree many times throughout the years I attended boarding school – from the ages of 7 to 10. When I was lonely or sad or mostly when I felt left out or misunderstood, my Guava tree kept me safe. A few of my friends knew about my tree and would tell others where to find me when I went missing, but most knew nothing about my hideaway. Only my tree and me and that's how I liked it. Because the orchard was so puny, not many other people ever came when I was there, but many passed by on the road in front of the orchard or sometimes came as far as the first one or two trees in the orchard but never came farther into the trees and so did not discover me. Not that the tree was big enough to hide me, just that the location of it was awkward to reach and needed some maneuvering to get there.

In fact, when I think of it, the entire orchard was awkward. It seemed to represent an earlier time and one that no longer had significance. It always seemed a little strange to me – like a place within a place and something that represented something else, almost like a mangled monument of sorts. Maybe it was the very awkwardness of the whole place that drew me when I felt my most awkward in life. I seemed to always find solace there – as if we understood each other. That's the other thing about trees...they know things. You see, perceptions of life are relative and what seemed like a wonderful hiding place for me then would of course seem inadequate now. Like life itself, nothing is really as it seems. Life is always moving and changing and what we perceive to be exactly right today changes tomorrow and threatens us instead. So it was for me in the guava tree and, yes, the tree understood.

Let me describe the arborous setting more fully to explain what I mean. You see, the guava tree orchard was not alone. The awkwardness it represented was not alone either for I lived for three years of my life in a boarding school in the DRCongo. The idea of one's being boarded in Africa with its beautiful natural habitats already presents a conundrum of some irony. Nevertheless, there I was boarded with others of my age, and some younger and older. The reason we were there was in itself awkward.

We were White kids of White people working in that part of Africa as missionaries and we attended boarding school. I had no real understanding of anything I have just written in any real recognizable terms; however, I did feel the unnaturalness of it all from the start. The school was at the top of the hill and overlooked a valley. In the valley it was cold and damp. On the hill it was warm and breezy. Down one side of the school was a village. There was quite a walk to the village and we made that walk several times, all walking in a row, to watch the local people at church, in the village paths, with their families – kind of looking in on someone's life. The strangest thing to me was how they looked back at us – like we had created something at a distance from them and closed to them. That made me feel nervous...in fact, I felt nervous quite often at that school for various reasons and I always felt watched also for various reasons. We never really spoke to anyone in the village and on the other side was the mission station where other missionaries worked, such as medical missionaries. There was a clinic there for the boarding school kids as well as the station people and a church and some missionary housing.

I used to like visiting those houses as they had nice things there, good food, and games to play. I always felt boxed in however, completely powerless and with no significance. We would be schooled in the Bible and how to live good lives by the missionaries but I still felt like I was living inside something while so many others were outside; and being inside for me was not a feeling of protection but a feeling of suffocation from which I needed to escape. I did not feel part of the others "in the box" either and I definitely felt closed out from those outside the box with whom I had a more natural connection. This was not really my nature as I came to understand myself later and it was not how I had been raised in the villages by my parents. I really wanted to get to know people, to make connections, to have friends, like my friends in the forest, but I just kept feeling cut off and away from everyone else. I disliked the place intensely and missed my family beyond words.

I missed my mother most of all and the home she represented that was not strange and was altogether familiar. The home was never a specific place for me but had the right people participating. I never really knew where the place would be the next time I was going home, so I learned to not think about that or look for familiar things. I looked only for familiar faces and my mother's face was the most familiar of all. I will always remember looking into her eyes and that feeling of knowing I was home. I will also always remember her hands — a strong midwife's hands that were at the same time gentle and loving. My mother had the most beautiful hands in the whole world.

We were boarded however for three months at a time and then collected for one month and so on until the year was completed. And what I remember most of all was never feeling either "at home" there or accepted. Therein lies the world-within-a world — although I was indeed White just like the others in the school, I was very different. In fact, the only Irish kid there. And was I, in fact, actually Irish? Well, that's what my parents were so, by default alone, I was Irish and had to bear all that was represented in that difference: my accent, my clothes, my lack of fine things, my strange parents. But my own strangeness was only part of the overall awkwardness I felt there where we were boarded. Being called Irish was really strange to me - I was a forest girl, but no one seemed interested in my personal story. I was Irish because my parents were and that was that. Actually, my dad was born in the USA and raised in Ireland, but again, no one seemed interested enough to find out any realities of my life. They seemed to only want to label me for their own purposes, as I came to find out.

Even though I was only 7, I had already experienced "difference" in my life. I was born in the DRCongo, in 1960, just as the country, which was then called the Belgian Congo, was getting its colonial independence from Belgium. I was born in a village in the Ituri area called Bongondza.

BILLY, DAVID AND RUTHIE (FAMILY ARCHIVES)

There was a lot of fighting, and it became unsafe for White women and children as all were associated with the colonists from which freedom was being won. The mission sent us home to Ireland, but my dad stayed to help the people in the mission stations.

1960 (FAMILY ARCHIVES) US LEAVING IN 1960

I was just a baby in my mom's arms. My brothers were with us: one was 6 and the other was 8. We went back to Ireland, and it was 18 months before we even heard from dad and didn't know if he was alive or dead. It turns out he drove overland with another missionary so that he could get back to Ireland to be with us. There was a lot of bloodshed in Congo at that time. We returned back to Congo when I was 3. We were condemned by many well-meaning Christians in Ireland when my parents returned to Congo as they thought it was irresponsible of them to put us in danger. Ironically, some years later, as I will explain, that was not their point of view.

The Congolese Christians were so happy to see us back in Congo and they told my parents that they knew they must really love them as they returned and brought their children with them. We were happy to be back with our friends in Congo. So, God does love the world! Then we had to be rescued out again in 1964 when I was 4, as I will explain, and then we came back to Congo when I was 7 and left again when I was 10. Back to Ireland. Difference? I was only 10 and my life seemed to be a story of difference and certainly no roots in any actual place.

Back to boarding school days when I was now 7. Everything about this school represented strangeness to me and the strangest of all was that I was not like everyone else at the school although I knew we were all missionary kids. So, there we were, all of us looking different from the world around this tiny unit of a society, and me unlike anything around or inside – totally awkward. You see, the kids were "Americans", and I was "Irish". Those labels helped to sort us but not one of us really knew anything about either one. You see, we were "third culture kids"[1]…apparently not having a real home. And all of this mess was negotiated on a daily basis through various power struggles we all experienced to remain in control of whatever we had that could be controlled.

"Candy Cupboard" was one such controllable item; the big two-door cupboard in the sitting room that joined the boys' side and girls' side of the dorm. Inside that cupboard were tins of goodies. Each tin had a name on it, and we could take out our tins each day at a specific time and take a treat. The treats were provided by parents at the beginning of the term and the "rich kids" who had parents living an airplane-ride distance from the school could replenish their tins often. My parents lived in the Ituri Forest which was quite a distance away and could not afford the plane ride. My tin could only be filled at the beginning of the term and had to last for three months. The name tag on my tin was always a rough sticking plaster written on in black indelible ink that we had to have for all our clothes' name tags as well so that it wouldn't wash off. The plaster was care of my mother's nurse's supplies and did the trick well enough. My treats were also all gone within the first couple of weeks of school which meant I spent the rest of the three months coveting everyone else's tin and thinking how I hated rich people! Sometimes, compassionate parents would remember the little Irish girl and bring extra cookies for her along with additional goodies for their own kids. That was a kind act from them I knew, but it didn't help me feel any more accepted, just more objectified in a way… sort of someone to be kind to…and that made them feel better, I guess.

---

[1] Term first used by **John and Ruth Useem, 1950**

I found out years later these acts had been requested by my mother in the jungle who would radio through to another missionary station and ask if anyone was going up to the school and could they bring "wee Ruth" something because she couldn't be there herself.

How did the trees see all of this? I had my perception of things. You see, there are some trees that are wild and untamed and then there are the intentionally planted ones. The latter necessarily possess a designed history and represent hands and feet of someone other than the indigenous. The trees in the valley – yes, those were the weeping willows that cried every night and rustled softly as if to tell their story of days before. Then there were the pines around that stood loftily above us all and were not intimidated by anything. The wind would come up the valley and whine through the pines as the trees resisted the movement as if blocking its progress. Then there were the fruit trees – those practical trees that provided something to eat. But then there was my problem. Who did the eating? Who actually ate that fruit? And why were the fruit trees only at the top of the hill where the White people lived? Maybe that's what the Guava tree knew. I sometimes had pieces of blood orange to eat or stewed guava on my plate in the school dining hall which were the world's worst tasting food ever made. I can still hear the command, "You will eat all of this before you leave the dining room today. Finish it all and thank the Lord for it!" You see I had always been taught to eat all that was given to me as those around were starving. My thought was always, "I really have no need for this and would gladly give it to anyone…" Where was the logic? I remember sitting there the last of all – even after the table servers had cleared and the dish washers had washed the dishes. There I was, still looking at the stewed guava and thinking…my tree would not understand this either. She produces the best guavas there are and they need nothing added at all. So why this mess? And most of all, why must I eat it?

Interestingly, those questions stayed with me for many years. Who else ate the guava fruit? I really never received an answer to my question except one day I saw some local Congolese kids from the nearby village coming up the hill. I thought, "They're coming for some guavas and blood oranges!" I waited for them to come nearer when suddenly I saw the dog that belonged to one of the missionaries lunging out of nowhere and charging after the kids. As they ran away as fast as they could, totally silently but really swiftly, then I heard the yell of the missionary, not stopping the dog but encouraging the dog to go faster and "get them!" Why? I thought…I don't want the guavas and I'm sure none of my friends do either…why can't they have them? I thought God loves the world…?

Then I realized I was watching this from a guava tree away from everyone. Away from those in the school who did not understand me and away from others whom I knew I would never know. I did not think in terms of skin color, but I thought in terms of isolation, and I was really, really isolated. And I knew even though there were many more of them than me, they were somehow isolated too.

So, I loved my tree and sitting up that tree I learned many things. I watched many people and thought about many ideas and dreams. Then there was another tree…a little, tiny tree that could hardly hold me in its branches. It was in the middle of the cow patch outside our dorm. This tree was scary – not only because of its weakness but also because it was itself away from any other trees and seemed to know my own thoughts of isolation. It also stood right in the middle of where all the cows grazed and often the cows would come under the tree and my dangling legs would touch their backs. What a thrill! A nervous, scary thrill, but still a thrill! I was actually afraid of cows because my mother always told me they were silly animals and might just do something strange without thinking. Something wonderful, however, was when I also saw the little calves and jumped down to run around them. I must have been a strange sight when I think about it now, but there I was a stringy little, knobby-kneed girl who always wore dresses but didn't really know she was recognized as a girl by others. Running around the cow patch with the calves who did not care who or what I was, just that we were running around together. Were they wiser than we thought? Did they know something the humans were totally missing?

Then there was the killing mound – the slaughter pen. Every Saturday, we would run to see who was being killed that day. I say "who" because these were my friends, and I would notice that one or two were missing. As I had found more acceptance with the animals, I used to spend lots of time with them and gave them all names. The school had its own farm which I realized years later was to grow food and have animals to feed us. All I knew was that they were my friends. Pigs were the worst to watch. They screamed a lot and there were no electric nodes, only a knife. Chickens, goats, calfs, pigs. We would watch them all get slaughtered. It was the excitement of the week for many of the kids and for me it was horrifying. I saw all the blood and smelled the warm blood in the African sun and knew that the next day I would have to face some piece of one of my friends on a plate and I would have to eat it without question. I am now a vegetarian!

That killing mound with the smell of warm blood in the African sun reminded me of another killing mound a few years earlier when it was the blood of people I had smelt; still a very strange smell and more ending of life.

CHAPTER  TWO

FOREST TREES

I remember running back into the mission house shouting, "Come see!! Some funny men are coming!" Running close behind me was my best friend, Larry. We were at that great age of 4 together and I liked Larry because unlike the other, older boys (my brothers being among them), he did not tell me to go away or go home and stop bothering him. He liked me being around and we liked to play around the mission houses together. He also never said those perishing words to me, "You're just a girl!" To which I always replied, "I am not a girl!!" Larry did not seem to care. Maybe because he was not yet sure what being a boy was either. So, we were a great little pair.

That day, we ran into the house away from the "funny men" who were actually "Simbas"[2] coming to kill us all. The Simbas yelled out that everyone from inside the house had to come out to be killed outside. As we made our way down the back steps to the side of the house, we were told by our parents to stand close to them. Once I found my place beside my mother, I looked out and saw a line of Simbas in front of us: all heights and ages, facing us wearing leaves and skin dye – yes, that was funny I guess to a 4-year-old. What was not funny however was that, now, they were pointing guns right at

---

[2] https://dbpedia.org/page/Simba_rebellion

our faces and waiting for the order to fire. I looked up at my lovely mom and asked, "Are they going to kill us now?" To which my mother, full of faith, quietly said, "Just pray Ruthie, sweetheart, we don't know." My two brothers and my mom and dad and I were all lined up and waiting to die. Larry was there too with his mom and dad – in fact, 14 children were there, 9 women and 2 men; all lined up and waiting to die.

So why were we there? What had led up to this horrifying moment? It was called the Simba Rebellion – a named coined by the leader of the rebel troops, Christofe Gbenye[3]. The rebellion followed Congo's freedom from Belgian colonial rule in 1960.

Here we now were facing the firing squad in November 1964. Quite shockingly, the guns were lowered, and the command came for all of us to go back into the house except my dad and uncle Hector. They were best friends. They worked together, laughed together, served together, and most of all had the same fully committed sense of calling on their lives – one Canadian and one Northern Irish, but both great dads and both obedient servants of God. We all called the missionary parents uncles and aunts and so we really felt like an extended family unit. My Dad and the other missionary men had been held as hostages in prison in a city 8 km away that was called Stanleyville and then became known as Kisangani, after the break with the colonialist control. My dad and Uncle Hector were released from prison when the Simbas were instructed to target Americans and no other Whites. Although my dad was born in the USA, he only had a UK passport at that time and he and Uncle Hector, the Canadian, were released.

Interestingly, the sons of Uncle Hector and my brothers and I have met as adults and shared memories of that day. We had been all held under house arrest by the Simbas for 4 months while our dads were all in prison. Then our dads were released and came to be with us at the mission house under house arrest. Uncle Hector's sons have told

---

[3] https://www.nytimes.com/2015/02/12/world/christophe-gbenye-radical-nationalist-in-congo-dies-at-88.html

us that on the morning of the day the Simbas came to shoot us, in family devotions, their dad told them that God had revealed to him that he would be killed some way and sometime during the rebellion and they shouldn't cry because it was God's will. Our dad told us that same morning, as a family, that he believed God had told him that we would be delivered.

During house arrest, the Simbas would often come into our mission campus and take things: tools, food, cars, anything they thought they wanted. One thing they did not take was a small radio. That meant our parents could hear the news and what was going on. That morning on November 23, 1964, Gbenye hit the airwaves and told the Simbas that if they saw any White people at all, no matter men or women or children or adults, they were to kill them. In fact, his actual words were, "take their heads off!"

Then, the Simbas came in and told us all to line up to be shot. My mom always said that she looked up to the heavens and thanked the Lord when they lifted the guns as she knew our deaths would be quicker than if they had lifted knives.

So, they really said they couldn't shoot us, and they commanded us all go back inside the house and the two men, dad and Uncle Hector, they wanted to stay outside so they could kill them there. It was such a strange situation. Why couldn't they shoot us? My dad always told us that one of the missionary kids was sitting on the back steps as the Simbas were coming in and he was singing Sunday School songs. Dad watched as the lead Simba came around the corner and listened to him singing. Dad said the Simba stopped and put his head down and walked away. He was the one later who said, "Put down your weapons, we can't kill these people!" Had that Simba already heard of God's love? Was he now facing a reality he had been taught about but refused to follow?

The kids and moms and other missionary women all marched back in the house. One Simba followed us in and opened up fire with an automatic rifle around us all. My mom shouted, "Everyone fall!" And fall we did. Our moms tried to encase our little bodies with their own, but I felt sorry for the bigger kids – no one protected them and two of them were wounded. I was 4 but the youngest was only 18 months and no one cried. Then the gunman ran back outside. I can remember the weird silence and stillness after the bullets. Were we dead? My mom lifted her head from me and said, "Has anyone been hit?" My mom was so brave and the only nurse. Then we heard the gunfire outside and through the door cracks my mom would see Uncle Hector being shot and he fell to the ground. Then more shots as they shot at my dad then they drove off in their jeeps. I was so proud of my mom as she helped the wounded. Two of Uncle Hector's sons had been wounded, and then she ran outside once the Simbas had left thinking we were all dead — well, we were silent. Very silent, but not dead. I have never had trouble believing that God shut the mouths of lions for Daniel in the Bible story, as 14 kids remained totally silent that day amidst a hail of bullets.

I always wanted to be brave like my mom and while she was outside helping the two dads, I thought, what can I do? I decided to find a little corner and there I knelt in prayer, "Dear Jesus, come and help us. Please help us!" I was so focused on prayer; I did not even realize that no one could find me and were searching everywhere. Auntie Ione found me just as Uncle Hector's body was being brought inside. It was a very hot day and freshly spilled blood has a very strange deep, dark, moist smell — a smell of something gone, gone forever. I remember that smell and looking at Uncle Hector and knowing that dad's best friend was dead. Still, I prayed in my heart, "Jesus, please help us." Just as God had already told us, Uncle Hector was dead, but my dad was not. The bullets actually only grazed my dad's forehead but missed his body. One of Uncle Hector's sons told us later in life that his mom told them all when they saw the dead body of their dad and her husband, "Boys, this is like dad said God told him it would be. Let's keep following the Lord. Then she quoted the Scripture, "The Lord has given, and the Lord has taken away, blessed be the name of the Lord." Their sons have told us over the years that if their mom had reacted in hatred and anger, that would have been their reaction too. She reacted, however, in forgiveness and love. So, the reality that God loves the world has huge challenges for us.

So where were the trees in all of this? When the Simbas left that day, my dad, the only man left in the group, decided that the women and children who were not wounded should all head to the forest to be safe. I know now his worry was always that the women and young girls would be raped or tortured and that the young boys would not be stolen away. I did not think of any of that. I just knew that there had been blood spilled that day and that we were not safe. Then we went into the forest, yes, the trees surrounded us, protecting us from what was going on in the towns and villages. I know that only Pygmies know their way through deep forests well, so the shade and branches of those massive forest trees hung over us and prohibited anyone from seeing us.

Mom, as the only nurse stayed behind with Uncle Hector's body and tending to the two boys who had been wounded and one of the missionary women. Dad stayed with Mom and the group and my big brother, my hero, was put in charge as the runner back and forth from the forest group and the house group to keep in touch with what was happening – he was only 12. What a responsibility! But he would be fine; he was Billy, my big brother. Many years later, he became a school champion runner in Ireland, so that was actually a great choice for the job that day. Did the group know what a wise choice it was to go into the forest? The forest is a living thing and welcomes all who need shelter. Surely everyone knew that. I did and felt totally safe in her arms. I wondered why I felt so at home in the forest. Now I realize the forest was where my earliest and happiest life memories were made. Let me explain...

We lived in a forest village called Ubundu. I don't remember everything about our village, but I do remember our mud home with the leaf roof.

UBUNDU
MY MOTHER, MY TWO BROTHERS AND ME, AND MY DOLL,
OUTSIDE OUR MUD HOUSE IN UBUNDU - FAMILY ARCHIVES

I remember how fun it was to make the mud walls from a kids' perspective – once the hole was dug and the women poured in the pitchers of water they balanced on their heads, we kids would all jump into the hole with our bare feet making the muddy mixture that was needed for the walls. What a screaming delight to feel that mud through your toes and become a mud baby from top to bottom. Then the mud was slung onto the bamboo sticks which had been placed in the shape of walls with bamboo weaves throughout so the mud would stick. Great fun! Slinging the mud every which way and inevitably getting a mud pie slung on me by my brother David. He was the brother who always teased me. A small price to pay as I always admired my brother David as he had a big heart of love and fun and adventure. I always wanted David's acceptance and approval because even as a small child I knew this brother with the big smile and shining, warm eyes, was the one to follow   he was always headed somewhere. I didn't want him to protect me. No, that was Billy's job, my oldest brother and he did that so well. I always wanted to know that Billy was close by in case anything went wrong. I wanted David to accept me and include me as he always had great plans with plenty of action. He was the one who kept reminding me I was a girl – I think he meant that to keep a distance between us as he knew I would be safe with mom, so always sent me back to be with mom. What resulted, however, was really only a growing determination on my part to prove him wrong and to demonstrate my complete competence as a friend and dedicated follower, girl or no girl! What was a girl anyway? All my growing up years, I was surrounded by boys.

ONLY GIRL - FAMILY ARCHIVES

The only girl with my parents, Aunt Ione and her 4 sons, after Uncle Hector was killed. She actually had 6 sons but two remained in the USA for education following the Simba Rebellion]

I used to try and follow him into the forest every day as he would run and play with his friends – always in bare feet even though mom, the nurse, kept telling us that we couldn't be in bare feet, and we had to wear shoes. Of course, I couldn't keep up as I was only 3 and was always left behind. The other reason is that my best friend, Toma, had twisted legs, as a result of polio, and could only shuffle along on his little hinie. I loved Toma so I would never leave him. Instead, we would decide to go to our house and I would sneak into the kitchen and steal whatever had been made and give it to Toma. We had such a fun time! But feet, yes, now those always presented a problem for me. First of all Toma's feet didn't work and mine were soft. That was because Mom made us wear shoes, but soft feet are useless in the forest; so every day, I'd take my shoes off and try to run around as much as I could to harden up my feet so I could run faster and keep up with David and his friends. We thought mom would never know – but she always did as there was another little friend, we would all pick up in our feet called a jigger. That was a mess to get out and it was always dad's job to do it. I wondered about why mom, the nurse, never extracted the jiggers while dad, the builder, always did. His hands were always big and rough, and his fingers were not able to dig into our little feet without a great deal of pain for us. He would drench the area with kerosene to "kill off" the jigger. Then, we were always shown the "sack" of eggs with the explanation that, "… I will have to dig deep to get everything out". If I squeaked, he would always stop and lift his head and say, "Now, be strong as a good soldier of Jesus Christ!" My question was always, "Don't you think Jesus would cry too if you were digging into his feet? I do!"

My dad, now there was a man! A strong, stoic, tradesman. Eager to help, build and create. He actually had a performer's streak in him too that he never really demonstrated through his life. But his wit and humor were always there – his way of performing was to support his wife, the storyteller, and his children in music while he himself felt it was God's will for him to be serious, focused, and without emotional drama. Or was it that his mother died when he was 2 and he never had any memories of being cradled by her. Something he did not realize until he was 12 and in Ireland staying at his aunt's house with his cousins. One night, as his aunt leaned over and kissed his cousins goodnight, he started to cry. He told himself, "I don't have a mommy. I wish I did, and I wish she could cradle me tonight!" Both my parents lost their parents when they were very young, and that reality stayed with them their entire lives. My mother's dad died when she was 3 and her mom when she was 6. They both found it challenging to demonstrate love and affection openly although we knew as their kids, they would die for us. I always pestered them both as I, myself, could never get enough hugs and kisses. Maybe I was good for them, even if they struggled to respond.

MY PARENTS AND ME - FAMILY ARCHIVES

The question I always had was how can they show such love to others through their service for the Lord and then get embarrassed showing affection to me? I would just have to be the best I could be and then they might find it easier to hug and kiss me. I was too young to know their life stories of childhoods without parents. I would learn that their love for others was a sure example that God's love can fill us so that we can share it with others. I loved them both very much and now that they are both with Jesus, I miss them more than I can explain.

My mom used to have such fun with the women of the village. She learned a lot from them about how to cook forest style and all her missionary career, my mother could shine when other white women were lost as she knew how to use whatever forest materials she had to build fires to just the right heat for whatever she wanted to cook; make rice that had the perfect consistency to fill you like a pudding but did not stick; pound manioc leaves and peanuts and palm nuts to get her sauces and flavorings. She later taught many Congolese how to cook European style as well, so they could get jobs in the cities – she could even bake bread that rose to perfection …in a barrel! She also could deliver babies when all she had was a pair of scissors and a lot of prayer. What a woman! I always thought, I could never be as brave as my mother. So, why did she often look so scared? What could frighten this level of womanhood?

My dad could build anything from all the forest wood and even knew how to burn bricks made from forest soil and sand. I remember listening to the men singing as he had them working in organized groups on various tasks. They seemed to respect this white man. He always wanted to learn how to use what he had – he could even keep engines running when all he had was chewed, chewing gum to hold things together. I always felt my dad was distant, protective, and hardworking, but always on a mission for God.

I often felt isolated as my parents were busy and my brothers were gone to school or playing with their friends. My favorite times were with Toma as we would go where we weren't supposed to and watch others from a distance – I seemed to have a lot in common with Toma. He was isolated too with his twisted legs. No one wanted to play with him either. We made a great little pair of outcasts.

Then there was Choko. Choko was a tree monkey that lived in the branches of a tree right outside our mud house. I loved Choko and always thought, how smart! If I could stay up a tree, I would still be alone but I could see everything from high up. That began my tree climbing expeditions. I always felt safe, like Choko, in the branches of a tree. That also started by love of monkeys. They are the most appealing creatures in God's creation; never without energy, incredibly nosey, self-determined and agile. I learned a lot from Choko!

I learned a lot from my forest friend and the families of the village of Ubundu. While my dad was building, my mom was in the clinic, I was playing in the village. So many days my mom would come home and yodel into the forest so my dad would know she was there. He had a responding call that sounded funny and weirdly hoarse, but did the job. They would then come home together and start looking for Luta. That was my forest name. She would start through the village and ask some of the mothers where I was. They would inevitably reply, "Yeye Mama ni ndani ya nyumba moja kule." They would say that I was in one of the village houses and "kule" or "over there" was always accompanied by a tilted chin in the general direction. Never a pointed finger but always a pointed chin. Some white people never quite got that and would rudely point their fingers. How can you not know? I was inevitably enjoying some rice with one of my friend's families in their mud hut with my fingers in a little bowl of rice. One day, I told mom I wasn't coming home when she came to get me. I was still only 3 but annoyed that my rice eating was being disturbed. "Ruthie come home, sweetheart." "No", I replied. "Mmmmm" said all the village mothers in unison as only Congo forest mothers can say it, "now watch what the white woman does," they said, "this is why her children listen to her. " So my mom had to call me again and come and take me by the hand and walk me out of the village house, so that the village mothers could see I was not going to be spoiled. Yes, it does take a village, as someone smart once said.

We had left Ubundu (then called Pontierville) for Stanleyville (now called Kisangani) to meet with other missionaries and their children for a missionary conference. The conference was being held outside the city – actually 8 kilometers outside the city at a place simply called, "KM Huit " or kilometer 8. Most of the missionaries met there for that conference and some I would never see again.

THE MISSIONARY GROUP, 1964 - MISSION ARCHIVES]

We children spent time together but there were two hierarchies in place: MK boys and MK girls. I was at the bottom of the girls' stack because I was only 4 at this time and Larry was at the bottom end of the boys stack because he was also 4. Again, I found my outcast friend and we managed to have fun around the campus. There was a main house where the mission leader and his family lived, and it had an office and guest rooms. We were the only Irish family, so we didn't really fit with all the Americans. I think that is why Uncle Hector and Dad became such good friends with Uncle Hector being Canadian. Although many Americans do not really understand the differences, there are differences and Canadians are not Americans. We stayed in a row of rooms in a back house behind the main house and the McMillans (Uncle Hector's family) stayed in a hanger. They had more space. Maybe because Aunt Ione was American they were more accepted. Not sure. I do know that in the various interactions between the missionaries, my mother had that worried and fearful look and dad was often silent as he was overlooked in conversations. Yes, he was that tradesman. Useful in the time of need, but not necessary when thinking things had to be done.

OUR FAMILY IN 1964 - FAMILY ARCHIVES

That irritated me then and still does to this day. Can't people stop and listen and learn from everyone? So many missed the significance of my dad because they didn't spend the time to talk with him. Uncle Hector did – he was a Canadian farmer. They loved hanging out with each other and were quite the tag team when engines needed to be repaired and things needed to be built. My dad was always a humble man and would give all the credit to Uncle Hector, but I knew differently. I was usually around some corner listening to their conversations and watching Uncle Hector learn from dad as much as dad would learn from him. They were an awesome pair! That was when I decided that when I grew up, I wanted to work in trades. It was years later that I would learn from a new missionary couple (also not yet a part of the main group) that my parents had helped them incredibly. As new missionaries, they needed help with so many things and my parents were always there to help them. I was so blessed hearing that from Uncle Chuck and Aunt Muriel.

When my parents would never be overlooked was when they preached and sang. My dad was called to be an evangelist and that he was first and foremost. So, this humble man who experienced marginalization from many for much of his life, was the best Gospel preacher I ever heard in my life. His voice was clear and his passion overwhelming. Yes, here was the fruition of his performance abilities. Never an actor, always a preacher, but still could command the attention of individuals and crowds.

DAD AND ANTHER MISSIONARY BAPTIZING NEW FOLLOWERS OF CHRIST IN THE ITURI AREA - MISSION ARCHIVES

He always had the most amazing smile. My dad had perfect teeth. My mom always told me she fell in love with his teeth which always sounded weird to me but perfect they were. The most even and white row of pearly teeth I had ever seen. The work of an orthodontist? No, my dad was a working-class boy from Belfast. This was simply God's gift to him, I believe, as when he preached, that smile was "the closer". No one could resist the call of God through the mouth of my dad. Now, he could not sing very well, that was for sure, but he did play the banjo. My mother *could* sing, however. And when she sang, everyone would stop and listen. She always told stories first of God's grace and love and then she sang. She and Aunt Ione would sing together, "Oh my soul, bless thou Jehovah" is one I can still hear in my head. Aunt Ione was an alto trained at Moody Bible Institute in Chicago and my mom was a factory worker who became a midwife but could simply sing. No lessons, just passion. She was the soprano. My mom was also a performer. She was a wonderful Irish storyteller but loved an audience too. So, when she had me, she wanted me to sing with her. She taught me harmony when I was only 4 and our favorite duet was, "He the pearly gates will open, so that I may enter in." The other thing my mother could do that no one could ignore was she could laugh. A full hearty cackle that made everyone feel happy.

Once the conference was over, many of the missionary families left and went back to their places of mission in the forest areas. We were supposed to have left for Ubundu as well but due to all the fighting, the roads were not passable for us to get home. We never saw all those missionaries again as many were murdered by the Simbas.

Grace was one of them. She was a few years older than I so we didn't play together but I knew her and her brother, Stephen, as members of our MK group. Not long after we all said goodbye, they were shot along with their parents and all their bodies thrown to the crocodiles of the Aruwimi River. At least that is what we heard. Please, Lord, at least I hope it was a shooting and not a butchering with machetes. I have lived all my life with the question of why Grace and Stephen had to die, and I did not. I have never understood that, and I have lived each day trying to make it count, so I am worthy to have survived. Other MKs were murdered as well and many of our Congolese forest friends – Christians who were associated with the mission stations and the missionaries. It was a slaughter throughout the central part of the African continent. As a result, I have always found it extremely off-point and inaccurate to associate God's blessing with happy events or affluence. I have experienced in life that most often, God's blessing accompanies tragedy, trial, and poverty. So, what is God's blessing? Again, that question, "for God so loved the world..."what does it mean? Surely God intends our happiness and plenty. If so, why then did HE bless the world so entirely through the torture and death of His son? It seems to me that God's blessing and His love is so much more than we may at first think.

So that day we all ran into the forest away from the Simbas, I knew I would be safe. I knew it was the safest place to be. We also already knew and saw Congolese friends also in the forest. This had been their home since the fighting and terror began and we would learn that it remained their home for many, many years following. The forest knows that there are rules about living and dying and it also knows that breaking those rules damages the balance of all things. It is not tragic to be killed by a snake bite as that is the natural order of things. It is, however, unthinkable to be killed by another human being as we are all created in God's image to bring Him glory and honor. That is the ultimate law of the creator that forests understand. The trees stand tall and grow strong in honor of His name. The animals are sheltered and fed, in honor of His name. At times, humans are also sheltered and fed when the human condition becomes so horrific that the creator's rules have been dishonored and only raw natural order can prevail. That is the creator's balance and wisdom. Thank God for forests!

Names were being called which we could hear in the forest. Our names. What was going on? Something was happening. We were all told we had to leave the forest and go back to the main house and compound. Reluctantly, we followed in file and then saw a truly wonderful sight! Besides seeing that my mom and dad were still alive, the other wonderful thing was that there was a group of men there jumping off jeeps and trailers and with guns. Everyone was excited and agitated at the same time. All the adults were organizing things and people and decisions were being made on our behalf. It was happening very quickly. Suddenly, I was scooped up and placed by my mom into the arms of what seemed to me to be the hugest man I had ever seen. He carried me to the jeep and placed me on his knee. My reaction was typical for me. I talked and talked about the forest, my friends, Uncle Hector, and so many other things. I felt safe but suddenly heard that awful gun. Then I realized I was right beside a gun that was being fired up and down both sides of the road. I was terrified and felt all the hot shells hitting me as they fell from the gun. That was when Juan, as I only recently learned was his name, put his coat around me to protect me from the shells. I knew that Larry was there safe as well as one of my brothers. I did not see my oldest brother nor my parents. I did see Smudge the dog, running alongside the jeep and trying to jump in and being told to stay. I have often thought about that dog and wondered what happened to him. I have always had a soft spot for dogs since then as I remember the confusion in his eyes and the connection with us that was snapped that day.

My mother told me later that she was actually sitting beside Larry's mom, Aunt Thelma. They were keeping their heads down in case of stray bullets when something hit the side of my mom's head really hard. She shouted, "Thelma, I've been hit!" When Aunt Thelma raised her head to look, she could do nothing but laugh. My mom had been hit by a lump of dirt from the road, not a bullet. The two of them laughed most of the rest of the way into the town, relieved not only that it was only mud, but also that they and their kids were being taken into the town for rescue.

We finally arrived at the airport in Kisangani amidst a hail of bullets. We had to jump off the trailers and head straight for the open-bellied plane waiting for us. I have very little memory of the details of that moment except I do remember feeling like Jonah must have felt when he was swallowed by the whale as we all were "swallowed" by the plane. I have been back on that plane just a few years ago, as it has now been retired by the US military. When I walked into the plane as an adult, I could remember where I sat in the plane that day although it looked a lot smaller than it seemed to be that day in 1964. That day over 120 people were airlifted out in that plane. The pilot later told us that he piloted the plane again amidst a hail of bullets from the Simbas running alongside the plane. One Simba managed to shoot right into a gas tank on the right-hand side of the plane. As we lifted off the ground, gas was streaming out of that tank. The pilot shut down that engine and told us recently it was amazing that we made it to Kinshasa. He said that there was enough gas to start a barbeque when we landed.

Who were the men who rescued us? Those other dads who were still in prison in Stanleyville, were able to escape when Gbenye gave the command that morning to run. Why? Well many military were being dropped into Stanleyville - Belgians, British and mercenaries. Mike Hoare was one of the mercenary commanders. Once out of prison, they went to some of the military to ask if any would go 8 km out of the city to rescue all of us, including their wives and children, at the mission house. The group that agreed to come, we thought were mercenaries, but 50 years later, found out they were actually CIA men. They were known as the Makasi and had been in Congo for 5 years fighting for the US in the Cold War with Russia. Juan Tomayo was the CIA commando my mom asked to keep me safe and I had the amazing privilege of meeting him in FL 50 years later and his daughter, Cassandra. What an honor!

I do know that leaving the Congo in that plane left something else behind. Not just my friends in the forest both living and dead, but the forest itself. Since those early days in the Congo, I have always felt somewhat unprotected and misunderstood. Somehow what makes total sense in the forest means nothing elsewhere. What does make sense elsewhere has taken me a lifetime to understand.

CHAPTER  THREE

WHERE ARE THE TREES?

W e returned to Congo after the Simba Rebellion in 1967 and then returned back to Ireland in 1970. Our years back in Ireland became the beginning of another reality in my life – that of notoriety. We became the Congo missionaries, the rescued, and we, as "The McAllister Family" began to be invited to churches, community groups, schools, and organizations all over Ireland and the rest of the UK for many years to come. We sang together and played musical instruments; my mother told and retold the stories of the Congo, and my dad would preach. Many people came to Christ and many more felt they should become missionaries and full-time ministry workers as a result of the ministry of my parents during those years. Really, our family collectively and individually started to live through what has been called by mental health professionals as, "survivor's guilt". Why were we rescued? How can we ever live enough and experience enough to prove worthy of life itself? Along with that came the "fishbowl" experience of being watched by many people. The length of my dress, my jewelry, my shoe heels, the tights I wore, and even how I wore my hair.

My hair? Yes, that was always a point of great tension. My mother had wonderful hair: thick, black, wavy, and always bouncing off her head. Her punishment? Well, in this very legalistic type of environment, she had to have her hair tied tightly around a shoestring that was tied around her head. Her hair had to have no attraction whatsoever in case that would give way to sin. Me? Yes, well, what did God have in mind with my hair? You see, I seemed to have inherited my father's very fine, dark blonde hair, extremely straight and that hugged my head – no bounce whatsoever. My punishment? Hair washing every day and I was expected to grow it long – not sure why my mother's naturally beautiful hair had to be hidden and mine had to be long for everyone to see. Eventually, the 70s brought in fake curls and I started to "perm" my hair.

My mother also taught me how to sit in public, how to sit on a platform at the front of a church and how long my skirts had to be to avoid being "worldly". No makeup could be worn at all and no earrings and only a small ring on one hand and a watch on my left wrist. So, I made those count!! I first wore a watch with an animal skin band and then I discovered Swatch© watches – yes, those amazingly huge-headed and wonderfully banded watches from Switzerland.

However, a totally different kind of reality was happening all around us, similar to what we had left in the DRCongo. What we lived through in N. Ireland in the 1970s was horrific and totally devastating to the country, the people, the economy, and the politics. A truly divided nation, suffering extreme violence and hatred. What I learned is that people everywhere do not like to be dominated or oppressed and also that violence and hatred usually follows that kind of imposition. During those challenging days, my father counted that one year we had 385 meetings in the 365 days of that year. My brothers and I would go with them every Friday evening after a week of school and all weekend, every weekend. Those car rides were something else! We would pinch, shove, tease each other and every now and then we would sing...what wonderful harmony we had. My oldest brother would sing the tenor, my other brother would sing the melody, and I would sing alto. I remember "Cool Water"[4] specifically.

Then back to the arguing and chaos. What was our problem? The whole singing show thing annoyed us all completely. You see, Dad would take the bookings; Mom would decide what we would sing, Dad would decide on the agenda of the meeting, and Mom would create the musical arrangement. We would simply do it all. I still get very tense when I see a piano for fear I will hear the words, "Now Ruth will play and sing for us. Thank you, Ruth."

The problem was one could never say "no". I tried it once and saw my parents both with worried looks on their faces and my mother specifically saying to me, "Ruth, when the Lord asks you to do something, do it, or He might take your gift away from you." So, in fear of being made "giftless" I always said yes from then on, but dreaded it inside. Why? Because I hate performing music in front of people. What I actually enjoy is making people laugh! One very sad memory I have of finally saying no to my mother's request to sing and play was in the hospital when she had advanced Alzheimer's disease. My dad and I were visiting her one day in the hospital and she was her usual vacant self, until she suddenly looked in my eyes and said, "Ruth, love, away to the piano and sing for us all." Of course, there was no piano and we were all in a hospital ward so I could not grant her request – Ironically, I would have done so gladly that day, if it had been a possibility.

The memories I have of the Northern Irish people is that they are a resilient and faithful people – also quite stubborn and fiery. While we lived in Ireland for those years and travelled around the country and cities singing and speaking to groups of people, we heard many stories of people whose families had been decimated by violence in "The Troubles"; many people had stories of loved ones being shot or bombed; others had limbs missing and some children had watched their fathers being shot in front of them because they were police officers. Then the retaliation killings – both sides killing

---

4 Written by Bob Nolan, 1936

people randomly because some of "their side" had been killed. We all lived in fear that we would be next. We lived with bomb scares and riots, shootings, explosions, and car bombs every day. Army tanks were a common sight as were police in bullet proof jackets and using military styled rapid fire weapons while patrolling the streets. The police stations were completely surrounded by wire cages to protect from rocket attacks and police cars were unmarked. Every shopper would have to be frisked and scanned before entering a store and our main streets would have army barricades and search areas before we could enter main shopping areas. Of course, as young girls, it was all quite romantic having British soldiers joke around with you and look into your handbag and smile at you. I guess young girls can find romance almost anywhere! Some girls, however, who actually dated any of the soldiers were knee-capped for daring to be in love with the enemy.

One Sunday, while we were all sitting at our own family table and sharing a lunch together (rare occasion) we all jumped when a huge explosion went off. It was very close and for a few seconds we stayed still waiting to see if anything else would happen. Then my brothers ran out of our house and across the street to an elementary school campus. Smoke and debris were still flying around in the air, and we could see some startled and shocked young men coming out of one of the prefabricated buildings on the school property. We knew that every Sunday some young male teenagers would meet there in an army cadet program for training and activities. These were now the young men walking out of the building – some with their hands over their ears, some bleeding, all walking like zombies and their hair, I remember, was standing erect on their heads as it was loaded with debris. As my brothers got closer to where the explosion happened, they shouted back to my mom, "Don't come any closer and keep Ruth back! She doesn't need to see this!" I was 16 at the time. What they did not want me to see and what they saw firsthand was a young man of around 17 years of age whose head had been blown completely off his body and was lying beside the rest of his body on the ground. He and others who survived it were covered in nails as the bomb had been packed with nails and was attached to the door handle. The first one to walk through set off the bomb and felt the full blast of the explosion. Nails exploded everywhere and we found out later that some of those young men had to have pieces of nails removed for months following that blast.

As people milled around and the police and emergency professionals came, I started to think through what had just happened. Once again, I was seeing that death can come to us at any age and that no one is really safe. I remembered when we ran for shelter to the forest and the feeling of someone chasing us was very real. That was when I was 4. Now, here I was at 16 and still thinking, where can we go to be safe? There was definitely no forest around. My parents, always missionaries at heart, immediately followed up with as many families as they could of the young men involved in that blast. We heard news from them months later as my parents visited their parents and some of the young men in hospital. What I also learned was that violence was a reality in any country or place. While we had received sympathy from people hearing our story from the Congo and how we as children had been exposed to such atrocities, now here I was just across the street from our home in Northern Ireland and it still did not matter – here we were still facing senseless and hate-filled violence.

The other huge lesson I learned from my years in Ireland was that the struggle I had in the Congo to be accepted was still with me. As I have already said, I realize now at my age that I have never really fit in anywhere. I had thought I would, however, when we left the Congo and went to live for some years in Ireland. I thought that at last I could borrow the identity that my parents had in Ireland and find myself. From the start, however, nothing actually worked. My schooling was an issue because I had attended an American school in the Congo and knew nothing of British history or even currency. We arrived back from the Congo when I was 10 and I had to sit for a notional standardized exam called, "The 11+". As I said, I had no knowledge of anything British and there was no opportunity to explain what I did know about US history and geography. I, therefore, did not pass this exam but received a "borderline" grade. I never really understood what that meant in real terms, however, in actuality, it meant that the academic strata of education was not open to me. I was at that point destined for a trade education. If my parents had been wealthy, they could have paid for me to attend grammar school even without passing the exam. A school principal told them to simply not worry – there was a secondary school that would meet all my needs. My parents had no idea either of the system, so they went with the advice. I had always wanted to be able to work trades anyway, so I was fine with that idea, however, my mother had a very different idea. She wanted all of her children to have the chance of higher education which she never had the option of doing as she had been made to work full time in a factory at 14 just like my dad. They were working class kids and didn't have a chance at more education until they were older and went to Bible school. Then from there, my mom did midwifery studies but always said she wished she'd been able to go to university and become a medical doctor.

What did that mean for me? Mom wanted me to succeed academically and although she didn't have the money to send me to a grammar school, she wanted me to study hard and do as well as I could at the secondary school. Well, I did learn a lot at that school besides academics – I learned how to survive by sheer ability and I learned just how mean females can be. I had one friend at the school who lived across the street from me and who still keeps in touch with me to this day. For some reason, Carol found the strange girl with the strange accent fun to be friends with. It was an all-girls school. In some ways, that meant there was no competition for boyfriends and so on, however, it did mean that the girls who were in charge of the rest of us pretty much ruled. These were not only girls but girls from less than affluent homes, so they also knew how to fight – actually the fights were amazing! They reminded me of a fight I once saw as a child in the Congo. Two Congolese women, stripped down to the waist in broad daylight and pulling the "daylights" out of each other. Very scary. I think girl fights are always more scary than boy fights because they are so incredibly intense!!. Yes, every day, there were fights, not in the school yard, but just outside.

So, there was a very blonde-haired girl who was a real fighter. She decided I looked like I needed sorting out and she was going to do it. She had a group of three other girls who followed her everywhere, totally feeding off her negative energy and with nothing to add of their own. Every day, she would stalk me at school and then tell me she was going to hit me. I would keep looking downward and then would walk away. The intensity was rising every day until one day, she and her posse came to me and said, " Today, is your final chance! We will meet you in the soccer fields after school and we'll beat the tar out of you!!" Now, why would I head for the soccer field? Yet, they seemed determined that I would go there, obediently, so that I could be beaten up. Very strange! So, I went home and my mother was home that day which was not usual. I told her what had happened and I unleashed "Alma the fighter"!! You see, my Mother was raised in an even lower income part of the city and she not only learned how to fight but she was really good at it. "I'll fix her and all of them!" She exclaimed as we headed full speed to the soccer field together. Wow! I had no idea my mother was made of this stuff – but I knew now! The blonde-headed bully and her group looked up in shock at first and then utter fear as my mother went full force towards them. She raised her finger and pointed it to them and threatened, "This is my daughter. Do you hear me? If ever you touch her or even scare her again, you all will have me to deal with. Do you understand?" "Yes, missus!" they all exclaimed and ran away as fast as they could. I never had any trouble with that girl or anyone else again. Ah, so, things could have been so different at boarding school if I had learned to fight, is that what was missing? So, why did they pick on me? What had I done? And why didn't I fight back? Why did I let this happen to me?

I began to feel that difference again. I had been different in the Congo and now here again. Interestingly, I felt less different when I was the only little white girl in the village when I was very small than later in my life when I was among all white people and now among all white girls, so what does different look like? Goodness! Why was I always different?

Some of it I could not really avoid. I spoke with a different accent and I never really looked like a typical girl, I guess. My hair was always short and cut at a strange angle as, apparently, I would not sit still when my mother cut my hair. Later, when we could afford for me to go to a hairstylist, I still always had short hair, as I was told my hair was too straight and not very good for styling. There we go with "the hair thing" again - this time it had to be short, not long, as the long had been a failure. Was the short a failure too? I was also not allowed to wear makeup and fashionable clothes as those were not regarded as what Christian girls should do. Yes, that was another difference — you see, Ireland was really regarded as a Christian country, however, there were very different versions of Christian. I became aware that we were the odd ones who had lots of rules and expectations to follow. Mostly, it took the joy and energy out of life, but it was regarded as the right thing to do without question. I also spoke differently. In the Congo at boarding school, I spoke with an Irish accent I had learned from my parents and was jeered at until I changed my accent to sound more American. In Ireland, people would telephone our house hoping I would answer the call so they could hear my fake American accent. They would laugh and just hang up. So, then I worked hard to sound Irish again. Different? Yes, anyone who feels different knows exactly what I mean when I say it is very odd and difficult to experience this at any age but especially when you're young and trying to identify yourself and make friends. You also don't always know why you're different, but different, you are. Identify yourself? That is a huge challenge in life and as I grew up, I realized I couldn't always hide with my tree friends.

Two things I began to realize under all this pressure: I was actually quite smart at school, and I began to work my way out of the technical track and into the academic track. Not that I wanted to, but the school told me what was expected of me because I was smart. I always thought my dad was very smart, but now I was being told that smart people did not do trades but adhered to the academic track.

Well pseudo-academic track. I would discover later that some ground just could not be made up, but I could change the trajectory of my education with good grades.

The second thing I realized was that I was athletic. I began to compete in gymnastics, track and field and became the Captain of the "Elizabeth House" at school. That year, we won the track and field trophy. I realized what many people realize when they are in an oppressive situation, if you find something you're good at, do that as much as you can, and people will notice you and accept your talent. I spent most of my time at school from that point on in the gym, working out, practicing, and helping the teachers with set up and clean up. I had found an identity! Always, however, I wondered how I could serve God in every situation. My parents had raised me to be aware of the calling on my life and that was now fueled with incredible guilt that I was even alive as I could never forget my friends in Congo who had been slaughtered.

So, I began to look around and realized that there was no Christian club, so I started one. Kim became a great friend who enjoyed that club. Then I started a girl's music group. At one point in my brief secondary school career, I was house captain, leader of the Christian Union and lead singer of a girls' singing group. I did not really know it then but that became a normal life condition for me – total busyness. It remains with me until this day – there is a comfort in staying busy when life does not make sense and also when it is so fragile. I had learned so much earlier on in my life that life is very brief, and I began to live as if chased by the gathering storm of possible death. Those days in Northern Ireland brought us death every single day – senseless killing and shameless terror. We even missed days of school for bomb threats. I have to say, however, those became a handy vehicle for those wanting to miss an exam or two. Mostly, however, it was no laughing matter. Death was all around us.

So being three wee girls who sang with their guitars and their bongo drums was quite a bit of fresh air. In fact, we began to receive bookings around churches in N. Ireland as "Karen, Sharon, and Ruth". We sang trendy songs and songs of groovy young Christians such as

"I wish we'd all been ready[5]" and many scripture-in-song tunes that had become quite popular back then in the 70s such as, "The Law of the Lord is Perfect". As I began to move into the Christian club and musical group, I began to then make actual friends. Girls that seemed to like me but mostly, did not laugh at me and who really enjoyed our being together. What was the difference? What was happening? Was this something to do with Christ? Was music becoming a positive identifier in my life? To this day, Carol and Kim and Karen and I stay in touch thanks to new technology and the friendships we made in school years ago.

Coffee houses were springing up around churches for young people and we were slowly moving away from our parents more militaristic version of Christianity that sang "Onward Christian Soldiers" to a more cozy, softer rendition that still threatened doom to those who did not receive Christ, but the message was much more relational and inviting. We even had a visitor in Belfast all the way from somewhere in the US. His name was Arthur Blessitt and he walked around the city of Belfast bringing Christ's message of peace by shouldering a huge cross and handing out fluorescent happy-faced stickers that read, "Smile, Jesus loves you!" While we laughed at Arthur as a crazy American here to solve our issues when he "hadn't the foggiest idea" of anything. Still, there was a quiet, hippy-like aura around this man that people felt. While he didn't actually say, "peace man", he did say "peace through Christ" and somehow the message was just as warm. Of course, we loved his stickers, as fluorescent anything was for sure. Those were indeed the "groovy days". Fluorescent, shaggy, baggy and platformed: all entirely cool. We also loved all things American: Love Song, Second Chapter of Acts, and any European who had an American sound like Evie, Choralerna, and Len Magee. I remained fascinated by all things American and still wanted so badly to fit in with them all. As I realized more and more

---

[5] Songwriter: Larry Norman
I Wish We'd All Been Ready lyrics © Ordure Blanc Music

that being Irish was not something I was able to do well, I opted for the American sound.

Thanks to the encouragement of my brother, I started singing as the lead singer of a music group. Now my brother was taking me everywhere to sing and he was our sound guy. I finally found something he and I did together - music! I was always working on sounding American, so my vibrato was smoother, my range bigger, and always with subtle harmony. The "American" sound was trendy then in Gospel music and I thought, I know about the American sound - I sang with Americans in Congo. At least I knew what the accent was like. Also, my singing star was Karen Carpenter.

There were other local Irish singers whose sound was different but mine was decidedly American. One really cool reality was that we were able to record vinyls or LPs as we called them. It is amazing how many wonderful musicians and recording artists we worked with over those years that The McAllister Family was being booked everywhere - we even were invited to sing in the US and were booked for several TV shows and to sing with The Gaithers. As they had double booked, that did not work out but we did sing with another group well known at that time - the discovery of the USA as a teenager was something that seemed to strengthen a strong thread of identity in my life. A thread that was becoming increasingly positive. It was also many years later that I actually realized the picture for the solo album sleeve I had made as a teenager was taken with trees and leaves all around me. Still the trees were keeping me safe. All of the albums were recorded at Shalom Recordings in Portadown, Northern Ireland and can be heard on YouTube. com under the heading "McAllister Family Music".

Yes, music has always been in our family. My mom's sister, Annie, was also a beautiful singer and so were her parents. Her sister Mollie could sing well too. In fact, her dad, my grandfather used to make harps and it is interesting how music has stayed in our family throughout the years.

ALBUM COVERS - SHALOM RECORDINGS, PORTADOWN, N. IRELAND.]

Music brought me great friends at school and around various churches and coffee shops. I was truly finding an identity. I thought maybe I am American, then, rather than Irish….is that what the real me is? I still thought that living in Switzerland and Canada was something I wanted to do as well but should I head to the US? What about all my friends in the Congo? I had been spared, I couldn't forget that. I was sure Congo was where I should head. What about my newly realized identity though? What should I do? I was only 18 but really struggling with following Jesus when I didn't even have a strong idea of who I was. Yet, I was beginning to realize that maybe it was what I was looking to, for that identity, that was falling short.

CHAPTER  FOUR

LOOKING FOR TREES

It was extremely difficult for me when I realized we would not be headed back as missionaries to the DRCongo. It was an idea that had been implanted in my mind since I was old enough to think about it and as a result of being spared from death when so many of my friends had been slaughtered. When I would become an adult, I would be headed back to the Congo as a missionary. Why? Well, it was difficult to rationalize not going, being raised by Bob and Alma McAllister. In fact, the very first day my mother saw Andy who would later become my husband, as a young man walking beside me, she asked him two questions immediately: "Are you saved?" "Are you going to be a missionary?" As he was interested in going on a date with me, he did not want to disappoint my mother, so he said "yes" to both!

Let me go back a little ways to explain the context of that first meeting. So, we, as The McAllister Family, were invited to sing and speak at a well-known missionary convention in Edinburgh, Scotland. This rather large gathering of Christians was organized by a homeland mission organization. This was an entity that organized and trained young people to become "homeland missionaries" around the United

Kingdom and Ireland. Later they would expand to Europe and Canada. Their training college was in Edinburgh as well. So, we, the McAllister Family, were the missionary speakers and singers. To me, this would be another boring event to endure. I was "Ruth McAllister" and had to sit, stand, walk, and dress accordingly as I have already explained. So here we were headed to a big convention in Scotland. One detail at this convention was that because I was now 18, my mother allowed me to attend the youth meetings and to actually dorm with some young teenage girls instead of staying with my parents. I have to confess, this made the entire idea more bearable.

As I entered the huge foyer of that beautiful church building, I happened to turn my head to the left and saw a young man walking up the large, stone, curved stairwell up to the balcony area. I stopped breathing immediately and stared. His hair was kind of very dark brown and he had baggy-legged pants (trousers) and a red sweater. He seemed to climb the stairs as if he had an actual goal in mind. I thought I had never seen anyone so handsome and lovely. Then, I thought, "... he must be the son of the president of the college or something. That's why he walks in such a confident manner. Ok, so forget it...he'll never be interested in me."

Later that evening, I described him to my dorm friends, and they laughed. "Oh Ruth! Forget him, he's never going to be bothered with you. Let's just have fun and never mind him!" We did see him here and there the next day and I pointed him out to my friends. Again, I was encouraged by them to ignore him. I couldn't, however. I thought he was amazing and I wanted to speak with him. Just to hear his voice; just to look into his eyes; just to be close to him.

The next day there was a "bus run" organized by the conference leadership. There were three buses scheduled to take anyone who wanted to on a tour of Edinburgh city. I told my friends that I wouldn't be going as it would only be for the old folks.

As we couldn't really think of anything else to do instead, however, we decided to go after all. As usual, although we arranged to meet at the bus stop, I was late. I ran to the buses and was told by the driver of the first bus that it was full and to go to the second bus. At that bus, the driver told me his bus was also full but to check the third bus…"and hurry! We're leaving in two minutes!" I ran to the third and final bus and the driver said, "I have one seat left. Get on quick!" As I made my way down the aisle of the bus, I could see my two dorm friends making much exaggerated hand motions for me to sit down in the one empty seat in front of them. As I came closer, I could see the seat was beside HIM! Oh, my goodness! My breath stopped again! I sat down and heard the smothered giggles of my friends behind me. I also glanced across the aisle and saw my parents! My mother leaned forward and stared at me with that all-knowing look of "I'm watching you, my girl! Behave!" I also heard, ringing in my head, words my mother had spoken to me repeatedly, "Listen! Never chase a man! It's not worth it! Any man that's worth his salt, will chase you. Be hard to get!" So, here I was sitting beside the loveliest guy I had ever seen and now I'm to be "hard to get". So, I thought I'd wait until I heard him speak first. It seemed like forever, but in a few minutes, he opened a bag of potato crisps (chips in the USA) and said, "Would you like one?" "Yes!" I responded. I grabbed a crisp and nearly choked swallowing it - yuck! Salt and vinegar! Hate that flavor but who cares, he spoke! Now I was clear and had been "hard to get'. He began asking me questions about me, my life, my interests. Then I asked him some questions. No, he wasn't the principals' son. He was from Yorkshire. He did not have a "hoity toity" accent (which I had presumed he would have and which I would have to tolerate and get used to and was determined I would because he was so lovely). He had the warmest voice and was really funny! Most of all, he had the most amazing eyes I had ever seen.

Yes, Andy and I got married three years later. Just in our twenties without any clue about much except that we loved each other deeply and wanted to serve God together. That in itself was, again, another trip down "identity lane". My parents and friends were not keen on my marrying an English guy, given the very distinct English/Irish history of violence and oppression. Also, Andy's parents did not want their son to marry a "traveler". "All

Irish are travelers, and she won't know how to make a home." I guess they did sense fairly early on that I did not have the roots they were familiar with. What they didn't know, however, was that I knew about trees and how trees of many different kinds can live together in harmony.

Only a small number of Andy's family came to the wedding. They were afraid to come to Ireland as in 1981, the Troubles were still happening. Having English accents was not particularly safe then, so I don't blame them. His parents and his brother came and his sister-in-law was one of my bride's maids. Interestingly, one week before our wedding, his parents were still not planning to come as his mother was adamant that it was not God's will. My mother, even with her own reservations about the union, called his mother and asked, "Don't you think God would tell Andy and Ruth if it wasn't his will?" Then she also asked, "They will be married whether you're there or not, but what will you tell your grandchildren the reason you weren't at their parents' wedding?" That last question sealed the deal and Andy's parents both came. Andy had his brother and his best friend as attendants, and I had my two sisters-in-law and Andy's sister-in-law and my second cousin whom I loved so much like the little sister I never had. I also had another second cousin as a flower girl. With it being the wedding of Ruth McAllister, my brothers played the trumpets, and we had some classical organ music played by, Sam, a friend of my brother's and two very well-known singers sang. The music theme definitely was present at our wedding.

PHOTOGRAPHY BY KENNETH NEIL, BELFAST]

What was incredibly interesting and, I believe, a God point in my life was that Andy was from a well-established Yorkshire family. A family that had been landowners, farmers, coal miners, stone masons, and landscape gardeners for many generations. It is interesting that the Lord guided me, the forest girl, to marry a well rooted English guy. What did he want to teach us both?

When a friend from church who was a travel agent suggested we go to Florida, USA, for our honeymoon as it was on special offer, I was ecstatic! So, even if we had to live in Ireland, I could visit my new-found musical identity for a short 2 weeks on honeymoon. Why did we have to stay in Ireland? Well, my parents returned to Zaire, as it was called then, to continue their missionary work and gave us their house in Moira, Co. Armagh, to live in, rent free. So, it seemed to be what we should do - rent free is always a good reason! Also, interestingly, while between my mother and my school I was not permitted to pursue work in the trades, this man I married was, in fact, a stone mason. so, some parts of the "life picture" were coming full circle. Andy's father had given him a second-hand van and one load of stone as a wedding present. Then Andy set up "Natural Stone Fireplaces" as a business in

Moira. It was a fashionable item then and Andy was really good at it. In fact, I came to learn later that his father was not so upset about the Irish traveler as much as he was that she was taking his best stonemason away from their family business, "Yorkshire Stone Fireplaces" in Altofts, W. Yorkshire. That I could see as Andy was extremely talented at designing and constructing these room center pieces as they then were.

ONE OF ANDY'S FIREPLACE DESIGNS - NATURAL STONE FIREPLACES, MOIRA, CO ARMAGH, N. IRELAND

So, while living in Moira, we had our first two children - a girl and then a boy. Having a girl first was miraculous to me. As I have explained, being a girl was burdensome as a young child as I was surrounded by boys and never seemed to fit it. So, I really thought I would not be able to have a girl. I thought that I wouldn't know how to have a girl. Yes, I did listen to Biology lessons at school, but emotionally, I was still stranded in my little girl's fears. Yet, we had a beautiful baby girl first and then we had a boy. I really thought I must be good at this - we have one of each! That's amazing!

What was a huge challenge was that I was still a student and now a young mother.

God had something to remind me though. My mom was a midwife, as I have explained, yet she was returning to Zaire at God's call just one month before I was due to deliver my first baby. I could not understand that. Why? First of all, I was not a girl that babysat other people's children as we were traveling around so much singing. I really did not know what to do with a baby. Also, I had heard my mother's "war stories" of deliveries and how serious things had gone wrong. I really needed my mother, why was God taking her from me? That morning when we were saying goodbye to my parents, the Lord spoke clearly to me, "Tell me what worries you and I won't let you fall." Psalm 55:22 CEV. I had to do that - I had no other option. What was God teaching me? Somehow, I felt that I was one step closer to understanding the reality of God and in relation to my life. I had to live a few years more to really understand that moment...

As I have mentioned, it turned out I was quite good at school. However, I really could not deal with the oppression, the strict uniforms, the rules and regulations even though I was House Captain and I was also a prefect. That meant I was "on duty" watching the really challenging behavior of some of the younger grades. At that time, you could leave school at 16. I came home and told my family I was leaving school. My brother, David, had a long discussion with me about my future. During that discussion he said, "What do you want to be when you're older?" I knew I couldn't say, "a trades worker", so I said, "I'm not sure but I think a school teacher or something like that." To which my brother replied, "Well, I hate to tell you, Ruth, but you can't leave school at 16 and become a school teacher." I was horrified. Why? Then as we talked, he suggested I think about going to a community college for my final years of schooling and to complete my A Levels so I could get to university as mom wanted for us all. That was a relief! So, I did leave school and went to the College of Business Studies in Belfast to complete two A levels -History and English Literature, so that I could apply to university. Yes, I started a Christian Union there too and began networking with Youth for Christ to invite some popular Christian singers over from England.

It was there that for the first time, I was taught by a Catholic teacher who asked me what I thought about various novels we were reading. No one had ever asked me what I thought about anything. I was expected to simply remember what I was told. I was shocked that my opinion mattered. He also revealed what had been left out of my education so far in my secondary school and that was the "other side" of the story of Ireland. It was then I began to realize that much of what we learned in organized educational institutions is controlled by the cultural and political context within which we live. So, I wanted to learn more, and I applied and was accepted into Queens University in Belfast. Some of my friends did not think I would ever be accepted as it is a prestigious university and there I was a forest girl, secondary school-educated and high school completion in a community college. Accepted I was and received an honors degree in English Literature and Language. My brothers also studied and graduated from Queens; one in Agriculture and one in Theology. So, my mother had her wish - we all went to university. Although she had hoped one of us would be a medical doctor as she had always wanted to be.

So, I was completing my final year of university while pregnant with my first child. That was an experience for sure. My oldest brother, Billy, told his wife, Norma, that they would have to return from Congo and be at home for a bit to help Ruth through this first pregnancy because he thought she probably did not know very much about babies. Wow! How right he was! My sister-in-law, the midwife, taught me so much! Great idea my brother had and there he was protecting me again. My brothers have been there so many times over the years just in the nick of time. Even though we have never lived in the same county since we were teenagers, we have still stayed close as a family. I am blessed that my sisters in law have been like the sisters I never had growing up. If I had known them earlier in my life, I may have understood so much more so much sooner.

Later, after we had had our second child and I was now teaching piano from home as a mom with two very young children, my husband began to feel a call to full time ministry. By this stage, he had also completed a certificate program in trades, so I had assumed we would be staying in N. Ireland for him to build up his business. He already had

2 people working for him and his work was amazing. Yet here he was telling me he was feeling called to ministry. We were both very much involved in our local church in youth ministry and Sunday School, but this was something more. What was that second question my mother asked him that day to which he said yes? So, it must be missionary work. I was fine with that - the rootless forest girl still had Switzerland and Canada on her traveling list. She also still felt that someday she would return to Congo to live for the lives that had been taken. At that time, I did not realize that was my emotional reality, not necessarily God's will for my life.

When we told our pastor that we felt called into full time ministry, he told us clearly that we should go to Bible College in Europe, not in the UK, as he said he really believed God was calling us away from the UK. That was a shock! Was it that obvious that we didn't belong there? What amazed me was that Andy, that guy with the confident walk, did not even falter. He applied to a European Bible College straight away and off to Germany we went. What about Switzerland? Well the college was in a small village called Büsingen which is in Germany but right on the border with Switzerland - God had heard my little heart after all.

As a teen, I always said I wanted to live in Switzerland to see the mountains. I can understand that as the Swiss Alps are the most beautiful mountains I have ever seen to this day. However, God had much more in store for me in Switzerland than enjoying mountains. I had much more to learn about my identity. The little town of Büsingen belonged to Germany when we lived there, but throughout history, it had been handed back and forth between Germany and Switzerland as it was right on the border. So now I was living in a little European town whose identity was also fluid, just like my own. Additionally, the Bible college we attended there had 14 different nationalities represented there in the student body and at one point, my husband was Student Body President. That was an interesting challenge as here we all were training to navigate our differences. Also, our third child was born while we were students there. A second boy. Now, what would his cultural identity be growing up in Germany/Switzerland? Our other two children were now in preschool and were speaking German as their first fluent language. I even could not understand our daughter when she woke up with a scary dream as she would explain it to me in German. I would ask her in English to tell me and she would lay back down in her bed in frustration that I could not understand her explanation. One thing I did realize quickly was that this, the home of fairy tales, had introduced her already to those stories with the angry wolf, "der Böse Wolf!" So, she was afraid to go into any forests anywhere - wait, my own daughter is afraid of forests? How did that happen? I had to make sure that trees became familiar and friendly to our children over the years since then.

Meanwhile, we really enjoyed the mountains and often went for weekend trips to various beautiful scenic areas of the Alps nearby. What was really interesting for me is that it was again a college run by Americans - just like my boarding school days in Congo. Now, here we were in Germany with Americans in charge again and now, as an adult, why was I being asked to relive this reality? My childhood experience had been mostly negative at the boarding school as I have already shared. I did have a very close friend as a roommate, Marilyn, and she and I keep in touch even to this day. I was going through my own insecurities working out how to be a girl with pretty hair and dresses when I was a forest girl with only one mirror and a small comb on my dresser. The huge challenge I have shared as well of working out what they meant by being Irish culminated into moments of being told I needed to be disciplined because I was Irish and were frequently "paddled" by one of our dorm parents who growled the words while he was paddling me, "I'll get the Irish out of you!" So, all I knew to this point about Americans being in charge was not very positive. Now, here I was as an adult, with 14 other nationalities in the student body and Americans again being in charge. We all were adult students and immediately, my musical abilities were used to play the piano for chapel services, voice lessons and community services. I was also teaching English to some children of the faculty and also cleaning stores in the small town to just help us as a family pay our bills. Andy, was a full time student and had his classes all day and also worked in local gardens and around the campus to help us all as well. In fact, we rarely spent any time together. Thankfully, the Rector's wife published a cookbook and with the revenue, paid for a young German woman to look after the children of the students. That was a huge help and yes, the Rector and his wife were Americans. So, what I was learning quickly was that one person does not represent everyone from a culture or country. Yes, there I experienced kind and helpful Americans who wanted as all to succeed and find God's plan for our lives.

Another interesting development, which I believe God used to continue to teach me more was that Andy was elected as Student Body President as I mentioned really because, I believe, he was seen as another "native English speaker" who could help culturally mediate between the various cultures represented and the body of Americans who ran the college. In other words, although Andy was English, he must be closer than the other nationalities to understand the Americans. As his wife, then, by default, I was also often asked questions about the American leadership and how they should be understood. Little did they know that this forest girl barely knew who she was herself and had a previously negative experience with "Americans". What did I know? Later in my life, I would also discover how confusing national tags can be such as German, French, American, English, Irish - well, I already had some idea of the problem of calling someone like me "Irish". Was it the same in every country? Did every country have a troubled history that caused huge identity challenges? I still had much to learn.

What Bible college did teach me was that God's children are all over this world and the students, faculty and the local community all became great friends and helped us forward as a family so well. For sure, there were very few trees around us. There were beautiful mountains and evergreens in small, forested areas but not so many trees around us every day. There were cows with wonderful bells that made a huge noise, alongside the haunting church bells in the town. We also lived beside the Rhein River and enjoyed its beauty daily. There were trees alongside the beautiful river. Actually, while I was trying to find the huge forest trees that protected me as a small child that were not here in this country, what I had to learn again was that trees provided different uses in our lives and here, as a young adult wife and mother,

I was learning that trees grow in various countries, look very different from each other and yet are highly successful in their purpose. Was that what I was also learning about people? What about me? Could I find a strong identity and live "on purpose" like my tree friends?

As Andy came to the end of his studies at Bible College, he told me that he felt called to full time church ministry. What? I thought it was missionary work we would head towards. So, he willingly worked with me to reach out to various mission organizations and each one did not lead to anything positive. In fact, it was clear each door was closed. Then something really unbelievable happened - my parents, who were still in the DRCongo working as missionaries and who knew we were finishing up Bible School and possibly heading out to Congo, wrote to us. We had chatted with them about coming out to help with missionary kids at the boarding school where I had spent those challenging years. I wanted to help other 3rd culture kids struggling to belong. This door would not close, I thought. I was a "home girl" there, so I was sure this would work out and I would be able to provide help to other missionary kids that may have similar struggles to mine.

This was before digital communication and so their letter took quite a few weeks getting to us but yet arrived just when the final mission door seemed to close for us. They wrote these words, "We have been praying and we feel that Andy should continue on with his studies and you both should follow the Lord where he leads there. We don't think you should come to Congo." What? As far as I was concerned, that was the final door and now it had been closed. Why did the Lord not want me to help other missionary kids? I would later learn that I still needed to learn some very important lessons about my identity before I could help anyone.

So, Andy tried to continue the next level of his education, a Master's degree in Divinity still there in Germany. We then discovered that internationally, education is not recognized the same from country to country. As the college was accredited through an American Institution, the German universities would not recognize it at the same level and would require Andy to complete additional years at a German institution before continuing on with a master's degree. We decided that with small children we would have to continue rather than repeat years of education, so it seemed logical to go to the USA. He applied and was accepted at an American seminary but a helpful administrator decided to give us an honest overview of how much everything would cost us as a family living as immigrants in the USA. We soon realized we could not afford it, so we thought we would head back to the UK. We found out they would also require Andy to retake two years of his baccalaureate degree before continuing on with his master's. We had no idea what to do. Then a student at the college who was Canadian mentioned that often people think what happens in the USA is also the same for Canada. She encouraged us to explore Canadian institutions as she told us we would be able to afford to live there with young children as immigrants due to their public medical and school systems. Andy applied and was accepted. Yes! That was the other country I always wanted to live in - Canada. Here the doors were opening to that amazing country. We went to Ireland for one year before heading to Canada and during that time, we recorded a CD together.

OUR CD COVER - SHALOM RECORDINGS -
PORTADOWN, N. IRELAND

CHAPTER  FIVE

LIFE WITHOUT TREES

What we had not realized was that this would also be a huge learning experience for us - God is always eager for us to understand who we truly are. For me that had been a life-long journey and now here we were embarking on a new experience as "foreigners" and again learning more about what true identity is.

I did struggle somewhat with this idea. First of all, when we would travel around church services singing and speaking as the visiting missionaries, I often heard people complain about their pastor or minister to my parents. As a result, I concluded as a young person that people do not really like their pastors and I told my husband that God could not want us to be in a ministry like this as people will not like you. Do you think I had something to learn? I also struggled because, although I had always wanted to live in Canada, I thought of it as a very wealthy country and I could see that people did not really attend church like they did in Congo. Why would God call us to a country where people did not really want to know God, or at least most people. Yes, I did have many things to learn.

In Canada we were involved in church planting ministry and worked with some amazing Christian people in establishing a brand-new church and also re-identifying another church that had all but closed. The areas in which we worked were truly lovely, but very suburban and no trees in sight except those that had been planted in small gardens in the area. The houses were lovely and what I became aware of was that, again, here we were in a country with one name but with many different cultures made up of even more individual people. This country, too, had a complicated history and many people in Canada still struggled to find their identity with so many new immigrants moving there. Our fourth child, our second girl, was born while we were living in Canada and actually, we had to head to the hospital in a raging snow storm. So, now we had 2 girls as well as 2 boys - I gained incredible strength from that reality. Here I was the forest girl who never ever thought she could have one child - that was for other girls who were strong, not me. Now we had 4 children and they taught us about so much. They were so full of energy and life and loved to have friends and share life with each other and always ready to try new things. We used to have a weekly "Saturday Snoop". Two criteria – they had to research and find a place we could visit as a family each weekend that 1 – had to be free and 2 – had to be some where we had never been before. Invariably we ended up in forests and beautiful natural walks - so lovely and they all grew up with a strong love of the outdoors and also of forests and trees. Our children also established us as a family of even greater diversity. Andy born in England, me in the CRCongo, two or our children were born in the north of Ireland, one in Germany and one in Canada. Here we all were growing together as a family. What was God saying?

Over the years our children have also taught me so much about life itself. Watching the joy and strong determination of our oldest daughter; the strong leadership and attention to fairness and justice of our oldest son; the faith and caring of our younger son; the creativity and entrepreneurship of our youngest daughter. As they have grown and married and had children, they have taught us much about how love keeps growing. Wait, so God's love is like that too? It isn't being shared but it continues to grow and extend to everyone - so now I was understanding more. It is sad when children do not learn about their heritage. We can see the threads of life focus, skills and abilities, and faith being passed down from generation to generation. There is an incredible life strength in knowing those stories.

We were busy young parents and as well as Andy being a pastor, I was director of a Crisis Pregnancy Center, and I taught ESL to adult learners. I then taught at a community college and worked at a Multicultural Center. During those years, I also presented at local schools on the subject of multiculturalism. Wait - the forest girl? What had I learned? Well being in these various countries, I had learned that culture is very difficult to determine as it often is evolving. In fact, anything to do with human beings rarely stays static. That meant I was no longer that terrified child up a guava tree but now was learning that I was an individual before God and could "belong" to many realities as life unfolds. The second thing I had learned was that it is very unhelpful to associate skin color with culture. In fact, what color is skin? We use the terms, black, brown, white, but no skin is really any of those colors. Medically, we learn that skin is a living organism, so it too is not static but living and often changes throughout life. I often began my presentations by asking the school children to listen to my accent and then watch me present and then tell me where they thought I was born. I knew that the English language, the "Irish" accent and the "white" skin would make certain suggestions to them. Usually, they would say that I was born in Canada, the USA, Sweden or Ireland. Never was it offered that I was born in Congo. Why? Well, the stereotypical associations had been made and in fact, incorrectly as most stereotypes are.

Also, in Canada, I pursued graduate studies at the University of Toronto where I completed an M.Ed. in anti-racism and intercultural studies and a PhD in Curriculum, Teaching and Learning. Andy completed an M.Div at Tyndale Seminary, Ontario. I am so grateful for this great opportunity to learn so much - living in the country and also learning at some of their best institutions. Andy was introduced to L'Arche[6] for the first time when he experienced lectures and presentations from Henri Nouwen[7]. I also had the privilege of learning

---

[6] https://larche.org/en/web/guest/welcome
[7] https://www.larche.org.uk/henri-nouwen

about bilingual language acquisition and cultural diversity from Jim Cummins[8], a well known scholar. The notion of cultural negotiation was first introduced to me by Jim Cummins who was Chair of my PhD thesis committee at the Ontario Institute for Studies in Education, University of Toronto (OISE/UT). I had certainly lived the reality of nothing standing still and culture being a fluid-kind of reality. Now I could learn about the theoretical reasoning behind this kind of reality

At our church, we began to have services to which we invited Native Canadian speakers, organized sporting events with Hispanic communities and I began to provide intercultural programs for foreign trained professionals coming to Canada, distance learning programs for language learners and intercultural support for various cultural communities in Toronto. Yes, God was leading, we were learning.

From Canada, we then were called to a church in the USA as I had been offered a position at a Christian university. Culturally, again, that was a shock as we were leaving Toronto Canada, and moving to Nashville, TN. Now, here we were in the USA - God had listened to my list as a little girl, but why was there another learning curve? In the USA, we have been learning much about diversity and Christ following. Andy has pastored and also served as a Chaplain in the states of TN, IL, NC and OH since we moved here and we also became citizens of the USA as we have lived here for so long. Each state is like a different country in many ways and often there are hugely conflicting ideas of unity and progress. Yet, it is called one country and it too has had a very complex History. Through our experiences in the US I have realized that even my American singing identity I thought I had was limited. Now, as an adult, a parent, a pastor's wife, a higher education professional, I have been again on a huge learning curve to understand who I am, as an individual. Now I was also wondering was that list of countries mine, or had God told me those were the countries my life would be lived in? Wow!

The entire ministry journey has been an amazing learning opportunity - understanding first of all what God's call really is. Like

---

[8] https://www.edcan.ca/experts/jim-cummins/

the trees, there must be a purpose if I am to grow strong and hold fast. I had struggled with being "called" into church ministry as I have already explained. What did God show me? He taught me that God's call cannot be assumed, it is to be heard and experienced. As we used to receive many letters from my parents in what was now, the Democratic Republic of the Congo, DRC, they always shared about how much God was moving and how many hundreds of people were responding and accepting Christ as their Savior. So, I argued with God and explained that He had led us to the wrong place - we wanted to be missionaries and serve Him where people wanted to hear. Not in affluent N. America where people were often too busy or too affluent to hear or even care to hear the message of the Gospel. Then God spoke to me clearly at four different times - yes, God has patience with us:

Once in the driveway of our house when He told my heart clearly that while it was difficult for the camel to get through the eye of the needle (Matthew 19:24NIV), it was not impossible. Affluent people still need a Savior, it just might take longer and be a more difficult thing for them to realize.

Second, God spoke to me during one of my devotions about the call of Ezekiel, many centuries before - I'm so grateful that God has patience as He must have had to repeat Himself often throughout the years of human history - in Ezekiel chapter 2, God asked him to stand up as he was being called. He was told to simply obey and speak with words of God regardless if the people did not want to hear.

Third, I was still struggling with guilt about Congo. I still was not really using that word to describe it but in later years I realized I was guilty that I was not there with my friends who had survived the slaughter. So, I was at a gospel concert at a large church in the community. The youth choir was singing, "Lord, don't send me to Africa." [9] Everyone was laughing in the congregation, and I was in tears. I said to the Lord from my heart, "Listen to them Lord all laughing and here I am I want to go to Africa, and you won't send me!"

---

[9] Songwriters: Scott Wesley Brown / Phill Mchugh

To which the Lord replied to my heart, "I know that Ruth, but will you stay here for me?"

Fourth, God spoke to me at the altar when Andy was being ordained as a church pastor. I heard the Lord speak directly to my heart and he said, "Yes, I am calling you too. Be quiet now and follow me."

God had been faithful and clear - follow him. It sounded straight forward, but as I have said, much learning had to take place. I am now so thankful that the Lord took the time to teach me. What else was I learning about trees? I had already understood my lack of roots could make me weak in life, not knowing where I was really from and not feeling grounded anywhere. But thinking again, those roots are in various places as I was learning. Different kinds of trees in different countries. So, was this another lesson on the various soils? Why would I need to know that? I believe God was teaching me the lesson of affluence – yes, I had wanted to escape into the world where affluence was not an issue and where my kids could grow up with very little and realize more easily their need for the Lord. Instead, God was teaching me the camel and the eye lesson – the bigger challenge of keeping focused on the Lord even when need seems to not be part of the awareness. So, if not need, then how would my children ever learn, how would I keep focused on the love of God – He taught me to understand His love not through a dependence on Him for the basics of life, but a dependence that emerges from realizing that in the midst of "too much" there is a need to touch the face of God in order to keep my soul alive. Nothing can kill the soul of a person as quickly as losing perspective and value through too much wealth. Keeping one's soul alive is a serious challenge when living in an affluent life context.

Later on in our ministry together, the challenges became stronger for me as a pastor's wife and then also to our marriage. I revisited my childhood challenge of not knowing how to look pretty like the other girls at the boarding school. At one of our churches, some women came to my husband and told him that I, his wife, should learn to go to the salon and get my hair fixed every week, I should go to the tanning bed as my skin was too white - yes they told my husband, not me. So, actually I was also experiencing that the pastor's wife, not just the pastor, was not always liked by people in the church. At one point, my voice was too high, my hair was too short, so I must be a lesbian, and I was doing too much in the church so that I actually wanted to run the church. God had clearly told me I was called to this as well as Andy, so why was this happening - again? My hair seemed to always be a problem and my skin was very sensitive, but too white? I had no idea what they meant. So, being a fake color was better than being authentic? This time, I felt that I had been learning some things in life, but this level of negativity was a shock to me. The church became a very unfriendly place for me, and I could never understand why God had made such a direct change in my life direction from the Congo to this. Why was I going through all of those insults? What were these teaching me about the love of God? Basically, that not everyone who calls him/herself a Christian has ever experienced the love of God; that the church is really a living thing and is the body of Christ not only a group of people meeting in a building.

What I did begin to see clearly was that while all of this was happening, God was still building his kingdom. We were seeing amazing things happen in various lives and much spiritual blessing. My parents, who had retired from Congo then came to live with us for some years first in Canada and then in the USA. This really thrilled me as I had missed my parents for much of my life. Not just in boarding school in Congo, but also in Ireland as we were always in the car driving to a meeting. During weekdays, I was babysat by relatives or my brothers. As I became a teenager, it just was life - Mom and Dad mostly gone and me trying to figure out life. Many people in the churches were blessed by the ministry of my parents too in these churches. Mostly, I was thrilled for my children who had time with their grandparents, learning about their story and their service for the Lord. I continued to pray that the Lord would guide my children to become his servants.

The music helped quite a bit with community outreaches and in-church contacts and concerts. Living in Nashville was a wonderful experience as a musician as I heard some quite famous people play and sing and every church seemed to have great musicians. Once, we had the author and composer of a children's musical come to our church to hear our church's children perform his musical. Our own children were in that group and others. We experienced much joy and blessing but also extreme negativity. So, if God loves the whole world, and churches are representing the love of God, why can some church groups become so negative? What I think I was learning more than anything was how amazing God really is. For all our human brokenness, God still cares that we find out who he is and who we are in him. So many human identifiers had proven to be weak and meaningless in my life, so does God identify us? Why would God identify us?

CHAPTER  SIX

TREES ARE ALWAYS WITH US

M iddle aged? I was now learning more about that journey as well. I remember my mother being middle aged and somewhat "feathery" in her emotions. I never thought that would be me, however. One morning I lifted my daily reading book from the bedside table, and I had to suddenly stretch it out to full arm's length in order to even see the words. What had happened overnight? I was suddenly my mother! Yes, that was in my 40s. No one had really told me – your eyesight really suddenly deteriorates in your 40s. When I share that experience with folk they all nod the head and agree – those who of course are over 40. Then I turned 50. What joy lay in store, I thought? Yes, there it was. You see my oldest brother has always been older than I, so he turned 50 when I was a young thing of 42. He seemed so old and not "clued in" to what was going on around him. "He's become a bit strange now that he's 50", I thought. Then when I turned 50 I realized, it's the hearing! Suddenly I could not hear people who seemed to be speaking directly to me. I saw their lips move, I knew there must be sound, but I could not hear anything except that TV in the corner of the room that no one seemed to want to turn off. Yes, too much ambient noise around. So that's why my brother seemed clued out – he actually could not hear us clearly! So, the next time you want to judge that older couple in the restaurant who seem to have nothing in common after all these years and remain silent at the table — yes, they actually can't hear each other! Then I came to my mid-50s, I couldn't help but wonder what in the world would happen in my 60s. I asked a group of women at a women's retreat at that time of my life, and they told me that when you're in your 60s, your knees go weak! The joys of the middle age years.

What happened in my 50s would change the rest of my life in a different way - I was diagnosed with breast cancer. If you have had cancer, you know what I mean - suddenly there is always something hanging over your existence - the reality that life is fleeting and ends quickly. I had already seen that as a child of 4, but now, here I was as a middle-aged woman realizing that again my life was in God's hands. Medical doctors have told me that they know that life and death are not in their hands. I experienced a lumpectomy, bladder surgery, an appendectomy, and a hysterectomy within a 2-year period. All of this taught me to keep trusting the Lord each day. Before that and during that time, Andy became ill with exhaustion and mental weariness. We left church ministry and, interestingly, it seemed that his experience led him into Chaplaincy ministry which is exactly his main ministerial strengths. I knew this, of course, and tried to influence him years before but God has his timing for everything. I do think our lives have borne that out for sure. Andy had many great years in Hospice, Life Flight and Hospital Chaplaincy work.

The reason I knew this was Andy's ministerial strengths was actually the reason I fell in love with him. I have already shared how we met and how handsome I thought he was. However, this is when I actually fell in love with him. I was visiting him in Yorkshire while we were still dating and Andy told me he was taking me to meet his friends. Naturally, I thought we were headed for an evening with some young people but instead, he took me to the home of two people he visited frequently. This was a brother and sister. They were both middle aged. The brother was a paraplegic and the sister had returned from the mission field to take care of her brother. Andy, who was 18 at the time, used to visit them every week so that she could have a break and go out to the stores while Andy stayed with her brother and fed him and washed him. I was astounded as I had never seen a young man of 18 in this kind of situation before. I truly fell in love that day with his heart and knew that God had gifted him with these gifts of caring and support. It was no shock to me that the Lord led Andy into Chaplaincy ministry.

Before that, however, my mother had developed dementia and my parents returned to Ireland. I actually went back to Ireland with them to help them settle. It was very difficult for me but even worse for my children who felt that they were losing their best friends in a deep way. My parents had been with us for 7 years and had seen the children go through many major stages of their young lives. They truly had bonded and really missed my parents. Here, now, with all this going on in my life, my mom, the nurse, was not with me - around this time, my mother went to be with Jesus.

So, middle age was not only a time when our eyesight and hearing became weaker, but also our overall health became weaker and then we had some major changes in ministry and I also changed jobs and started to work at home for another sector of higher education. My father was back in N. Ireland and my brothers were still involved with missions in the DRCongo and also had houses in N. Ireland. We were all still in the USA as a family and trying to make sense of getting older, getting used to children now being adults and getting married and having grandchildren! Who would have thought the joy of grandchildren - they really are perfect!

During these years, I would travel back to visit with my dad who actually lived until he was 95. We hadn't expected that as he had heart surgery some years before and he seemed so weak for a while. Now he was stronger and even though my mother had gone to be with Jesus, my dad was speaking at church services again around the Irish countryside. I remember my dad telling me about how much he missed my mother and especially her voice. He always said no one could sing like her! Another thing he kept asking me was why we had not yet applied for US citizenship. There it was again, the whole idea of belonging. Did I belong in the USA? Had I finally found my identity? As he talked, however, I again saw how this idea of identity was incredibly complex.

My dad was actually born in Germantown, PA. His father was
a carpenter as was his father before him. My great-grandfather was
actually a carpenter at the Belfast Shipyard, and had worked on the
Titanic. The Irish perspective on this was, "The Titanic was fine when
it left Belfast. It was that English captain that ruined everything!" So,
the burdens of history continued. During the early 1920s there was
little work for carpenters in Belfast and so my grandfather left for the
USA with his wife and their little daughter Kathleen. Not long after
they arrived, my dad was born and a year later, his mother died from
Septicemia as they had no medical care. As my grandfather still had not
found much work, he put his two young children in an orphanage and
went north to Canada as his cousin had a farm there and he hoped to
earn some money as a farm laborer.

DAD AND HIS SISTER AND THE ORPHANAGE AND THEIR
MOM'S GRAVE IN PHILADELPHIA - FAMILY ARCHIVES

For a few years my dad and his sister lived at the orphanage and
eventually his grandmother in Belfast heard about everything and sent
a letter to the orphanage to send the two children back to Belfast where
she would take care of them. The orphanage complied and my dad at
4 and his sister at 6, crossed the ocean in a liner. A group of "Orange
Men"[10] were traveling back for a time of celebration in Belfast and told
the orphanage they would watch over the children. I still believe it was
God Himself who watched over them and kept them from falling over

---

[10] https://www.britannica.com/topic/Orange-Order

the side of the ship, amongst other possible dangers! Their grandmother met them in the port of Belfast and took them home with her and raised them in Belfast. Some years later, their father returned from Canada and was able to help with support for them. Not only had their father not forgotten them, but the US Army contacted my dad when Pearl Harbor happened in WWII as he had just turned 18 and told him they would be conscripting him to fight for them in the Army. It turned out that my dad joined up one week before he was conscripted and said it was what any good Irish man would do - not wait for conscription. It turned out that my dad became Chaplain's assistant and served in the first armies of liberation in Europe. He even attended the Nuremberg Trials.

MY DAD AS A US SOLDIER - FAMILY ARCHIVES]

My Dad was so proud of his US history that he encouraged us to become US citizens which we did just one month before he went to be with Jesus. He was so happy that we did that.

My parents as a young couple heading to the mission field. Family Archives

My parents' grave in N. Ireland - Family Archives

What I was learning over and over in my life was that, like trees, our strength is not in having one set identity but growing strong in who we are and realizing that even when we think there are no trees around us, or in human terms, no one around us that really understands who we are, our life experience is ours to grow from, not to sink into. Trees do not grow strong in swamps, they grow strong in good soil within the context that best suits them. So, if I spend my life trying to be like someone else, I am truly missing the entire point of life. I am to be me. The strongest me I can be. So how do I become as strong as I can be? What makes me stronger?

CHAPTER  SEVEN

REMEMBERING THE GUAVA TREE

The idea that not everyone is participating in life from the same place, was impressed on me early on. Even earlier, however, I had another more violent view of racism and the anger and resentment it can bring. As I explained, I had watched, from my mother's side, as men and young boys pointed guns to our faces in order to shoot and kill us. As a child of 4, it wasn't awkwardness I felt that day nor fear, only inquisitiveness as I looked at my mother and simply asked, "Are they going to kill us?" That inquisitiveness has stayed with me throughout life. Why is life like this? Why do people do what they do? Why are some people not accepted by others? Why do some people want to kill other people?

Back to my friend Larry, also 4. You see, my friend Larry and I had quite a little world in which we played in the sun. Our parents, the missionaries, were usually busy with something: talking, planning, cooking, making something, inventing something, or just sharing funny or sad stories. Larry and I however, had a world of fun playing with "kufa" plants, gathering silver water drops in leaves, and chasing dogs around – especially one of the dogs belonging to one of the missionaries. It was a furry dog, poor thing, in the blazing Kisangani heat. We were having fun without realizing the full context within which we were living as children. We didn't know we were hated by people just across the road from where we played – people with guns. Our parents always spoke of people we loved and who loved us. We had friends with whatever color of skin – we hadn't noticed. But one day it was planned we were to die.

We all didn't die that day but some did both Black and White – those Black folks who were friends of the White people also died. Many more White people in other parts of the country were shot or cut into pieces. Many Black people were also shot or cut into pieces and all the bodies were thrown into the rivers – crocodiles up and down the rivers had feasts that day and other days as the fighting continued.

Maybe that's why I was so aware of something wrong at the boarding school. I had already lived through a line of Black and a line of White with guns in between. At the school there were places of White and places of Black - no guns as yet, but I couldn't help thinking, they must be coming. One day the guns will come and we'll all die. Some years later, that school was razed to the ground. The guns did come and people did die. If we had gone to the school as Andy and I had planned, we would have been killed.

The view from the tree, however, revealed to me that prejudice is more subtle. I was an outsider – maybe not in skin color......actually, my very white and freckly skin was some of the whitest in the school. Nevertheless, I didn't fit in. Yes, I was Irish by default, but I was also a girl socialized by boys who was more comfortable sitting in a tree than putting on makeup and combing my hair. I was more comfortable doing that, but I longed to have pretty things because I realized sitting in that tree that I wasn't in fact a boy. I was a girl and needed to know how to do other things, but I didn't know how. Instead, I hid in a tree and only came down to attend study hall or go to bed. Maybe that's why the dorm parent decided, one year, that I needed to have a very sweet, girly, girl friend as a roommate. Perhaps to take away the "edge" I had and make me softer. The problem was I was jealous of her as I couldn't be like her, so I took control of the situation and decided to teach her to do what I knew how to do well – pillow fight! My brothers and their friends taught me well. Instead of teaching her how to pillow fight, I made her cry and I got into severe trouble for causing her pain. I have never been able to cry on cue and have always envied girls who could. They seemed to get a lot of attention and I seemed to continue to be rejected. The pain inside me was left unattended and simply grew. Where did I belong and how could I relate? That dilemma stayed with me throughout my life as I have explained. What I learned, however, was that no one has a clear identity. Everyone's history is complex and requires understanding. Even the bullies are people who need to feel they belong somewhere, so by identifying someone as different, they all can feel they belong.

As an adult and a hard-working professional in several different countries, I also experienced that being a woman, even one educated in two very highly ranked universities was still not an "in". Many women have experienced similar stories to mine - being part of a male-dominated group means that you have to be smarter, more hardworking, and willing to not get the glory for your ideas, if you want to keep your job. My problem with that was I never could keep quiet. I always challenged the status quo and expected equality. Therefore, I was ousted, maneuvered or recharacterized in my positions while men continued to sometimes work at half pace, with fewer ideas and not as good at their jobs. I remember encouraging my sons to be strong men who worked hard but men who treated everyone equally and encouraged my daughters to never have to rely on a man in life or in work. Be strong and support yourself. I also trained my sons and my daughters how to take care of themselves, do their own washing from when they were 13, cook for themselves as needed and always clean up their own mess. Why? So that they would not marry because they needed to be looked after but because they were in love and could experience an equal partnership in their marriage. Andy and I have striven for that all our married lives. Now, where did I get that idea from?

CHAPTER EIGHT

THE WISDOM
OF TREES

I have discovered that understanding who we are has an earthly component and an eternal component. Mostly, we become disillusioned and confused when we think our earthly identity is all there is for the various reasons I have discussed in these chapters. Life is complex, everyone has a different story and life is lived in different places and at different paces, so how could there be only one identity. Additionally, we are from different cultures, different races, different genders, we are different ages throughout life and experience different seasons of life, so again, how could we have only one identity. The huge reality I came to understand is that we have a spiritual identity which is actually stronger, more secure and stands forever. That is our identity in Christ. Why don't we spend more time in life developing a stronger relationship with Christ in whom we can truly become known to God and helpful to our neighbors while still here on earth?

The Bible provides us with guidance for our lives and throughout explains how things began for us as humans and then how we struggled for centuries to try and find God and then how God sent His son, Jesus, to show us exactly who he is and who we should be as his followers. In fact, many choose to still live under the law and not under the grace of Christ. Why? It seems to me that people prefer darkness rather than light, as the Scripture says. We seem to prefer the old roads even if they are rugged and dangerous simply because we are afraid to walk in the light of God and show his love to everyone around us. Yes, the wisdom of the trees - they already had taught me how to grow strong, throughout my life I was learning how to become a strong person with a strong identity. Not through my own life experiences but through the new life I experienced in Christ.

How did that happen for me? When we had returned from Congo in 1964 after being rescued by the CIA group of soldiers, I was driving with my dad in the car one day and as a 4-year-old, I know my little mind was overcome and still trying to work out what had just happened to us. I asked my dad, "Daddy, what does it mean to be a Christian?" I will never forget that my dad drove the car to the side of the road and stopped it, turned to me and said, "A Christian is a person who has asked Jesus to come into their life, forgive their sins and to be their friend." I have to be honest, I needed a friend. So, I prayed and asked Jesus to be my Savior and friend. People can say that small children cannot make eternal decisions. Well, I did and remember that moment like it was yesterday. I meant it. That is when my journey following Christ began. Then at 15, I heard the voice of the Lord speaking into my heart and asking me to dedicate my whole life to Him. It is difficult to have well known parents, hard working missionaries, hard working midwife and tradesman and then believe that God could have a plan for little me. So, I handed my life fully to the Lord - interestingly, the verses that the Lord used to call me where, "But more than anything else put God's work first and do what he wants. Then the other things will be yours as well. "(Matthew 6:33 CEV). I thought that it sounded like a great plan, so I told the Lord I would follow him fully. What I did not know was that God would also help me to more fully understand myself and more importantly who I could become in Him.

We have often been taught about Solomon and how wise he was and yet we hear God say, "Even Solomon in all his glory was not arrayed as one of these." (Matthew 6:29 KJV) Actually, it seems that even though Solomon was incredibly wise and gifted, he missed some of the eternal wisdom that would have helped him through many of life's challenges. It seems that while we as humans try to have a sense of belonging to those around us, impress others, be admired by others, really, the main challenge in life is to be known by God. While belonging to a family is a basic human need, often humans articulate their groups as exclusive and closed to others. Sometimes those groups may be groups of children within a school where some are "in" and some are "out". It might be about race, culture, religion, wealth, or gender. Some are able to feel they belong, but it is important that others are excluded because they are different. What I have learned in my life is that "different" is what God intended for all of us. In fact, God is a God of diversity. Think of snowflakes and leaves, no two are the same. Now think of humans, again, no two are the same. Even twins or triplets may look very similar, but they are distinct individuals. So, God's vision is wide, diverse and yet inclusive. Human vision is exclusive, separating and closed. It's a "them" versus "us" idea of life.

So, human brokenness has a need and that is for the enlargement of Christ. God so loved "THE WORLD" - that means everyone. Jesus died for EVERYONE and ANYONE can accept him as Lord and Savior. When we do that, our identity and understanding of identity is not broken or exclusive, but open and welcoming. It is also strong. That is what I have learned throughout my life. Like the strong trees with deep roots - while I have never had an earthly experience of being rooted anywhere, I have come to understand that being rooted in Christ is a forever reality. It is also interesting that I have experienced a bond with others who are rooted in Christ, even if I have never met them before, or even do not speak their language. I know that belonging to Jesus brings people together, it does not drive people apart. Even some of the gender confusion we are experiencing in our society currently, can be a search for identity that can only be found in Jesus, not looking like someone else, or even a group of people. Truly being rooted in Christ brings strength or identity and purpose and unites Christ followers all over this world.

Some years ago, as a teacher of English as a Second or Foreign Language, I traveled to China at the request of a group of schools there to teach some teachers about Western methods of teaching English as a Foreign Language. The entire experience was truly amazing and I learned many things. I remember, however, feeling a bit lost at first as I did not speak any Chinese languages and I sat in my hotel room wondering how this whole project would work. I did have a translator and I was asked to stay at the hotel and a driver would be sent to pick me up each day to take me to the teachers I would be teaching. As I sat one day in my room, I prayed these words, "Lord, I know missionaries have been here, so there must be some Christ Followers. If you could show me you, I will feel at home, and I'll be able to relax." The next day, the supervisor who was responsible for overseeing my work there with the teachers had found out I was married to a pastor and so she took me on my "free" afternoon for a trip to a church so that I would feel at home. She drove me to a Catholic church, so clearly she did not know that Catholic priests do not marry, and met the janitor and told him (my translator told me) that I needed to be shown around the church because I was married to a pastor and she wanted me to have a nice afternoon. Once she left, the elderly man who was the janitor, turned to me and said in English, "You aren't Catholic are you?" I said, "No, I'm not." He said, "Neither am I, I'm just the janitor here and clean the church. " We shared a chuckle and then he said something I will never forget, " Many years ago, the missionaries told us about Jesus. I gave my heart to him and they taught us to sing (then he sang) Into my heart, into my heart, come into my heart, Lord Jesus…". I started to sing with him, and we were immediately bonded. Total strangers, from totally different life experiences, yet suddenly one in Christ. It was like we had known each other all our lives! Jesus was there for sure and brought us together as his children and as members of his eternal family. The greatest tree of all had been the reason we could be family - the cross of Christ.

If you feel somewhat lost in life, you are not alone. If you feel challenged to find where you belong, you're not alone. If you have moved around a lot or not had many string trees around you, you are not alone. In fact, the Bible tells us that Jesus did not come for those who have no needs, but for those of us who know we have many needs. We may have physical needs, financial needs, or other human challenges, but to truly belong in an eternal sense, we need Jesus. He is our rock and on him we can stand strong. Through him we can know purpose and a clear sense of identity in this life. Because of him, we can know eternal identity that will last forever. While we may still have to work out language and cultural differences and other differences in this life, we do not need to think that these human identities are the only ones we must work on. Our eternal identity is much more fulfilling and will last forever. Ask Jesus to be your Savior today and follow him for the rest of this life and into the next in his strength and for his glory. Amen! Or as my dad used to always say when He felt encouraged in the Lord - Hallelujah!

POSTLUDE UPDATE

My two brothers both had four children as well and all twelve of my parent's grandchildren are wonderful individuals and parents. My oldest brother, Bill's wife, Norma, was a midwife like my mother and continued in the medical profession and my younger brother's wife, Sabine, has been an amazing missionary and relief project manager in the Congo for many years working with David. We have a broad scope of teachers, doctors, nurses, business professionals, social workers, support workers, and international consultants in our "children". We are all enjoying our grandchildren now and continue to be amazed at how God continues to develop and grow them all. Interestingly, we are all still quite international with some families in Ireland, England, Wales, USA, Dubai and Switzerland. Yet we all keep in contact with new technology and meet up for memorials of my parents and weddings. What is amazing is that the family diversity again emphasizes the greatness of God and how his love extends across the world - everywhere! It is also amazing how the interest in serving the Lord as my parents demonstrated has always been front and center of our lives. My brothers have continued to support ministries in the DRCongo. My brother, David, was awarded an MBE by Her Majesty, Queen Elizabeth II, in recognition of the years of his work in the DRCongo. My brother, Bill, has worked for many mission and relief organizations and is currently working as a director for an Christian Education organization in Congo. I also work as a consultant on various university and school projects in Congo. We remember our earthly roots, but we know that our eternal roots in Christ are what truly identify us, and those roots and that identity will last for all eternity.

PHOTO CREDIT:
PAUL TSHIHAMBA, IMAGO DEI MEDIA

Printed in the United States
by Baker & Taylor Publisher Services